Common Mistake
Elementary Math—And
How to Avoid Them

Learn the most effective ways to teach elementary math, no matter how much experience you have with the subject. In this book, Fuchang Liu takes you through many common mistakes in math instruction and explains the misunderstandings behind them. He points out practices that should be avoided, helping you to adjust your lessons so that all students can achieve success.

You'll discover how to. . .

◆ Increase your confidence with core math principles and reasoning
◆ Set your students on the path toward eventually developing more complex math skills
◆ Improve student achievement by approaching problems in logical yet creative ways
◆ Overcome common challenges faced by students and teachers
◆ Teach problem solving for different learning styles

Every chapter reconsiders well-established ways of teaching all areas of elementary math, from addition and subtraction to statistics and graphs. Helpful examples and tips are scattered throughout the book, offering revisions to the way these topics are often presented in the classroom. Also included are group study ideas for principals and instructional coaches so your school or district can work on the book together. With this practical guide, you'll be ready to help students truly develop their math understanding.

Fuchang Liu is Associate Professor of Mathematics Education at Wichita State University. Previously, he taught high school math in Louisiana and Texas.

Other Eye On Education Books
Available from Routledge

Common Mistakes in Teaching Elementary Math—And How to Avoid Them

Fuchang Liu

Routledge
Taylor & Francis Group

NEW YORK AND LONDON

First published 2017
by Routledge
711 Third Avenue, New York, NY 10017

and by Routledge
2 Park Square, Milton Park, Abingdon, Oxon, OX14 4RN

Routledge is an imprint of the Taylor & Francis Group, an informa business

Library of Congress Cataloging-in-Publication Data
Names: Liu, Fuchang, 1957–
Title: Common mistakes in teaching elementary math : and how to avoid
    them / by Fuchang Liu.
Description: New York : Routledge, 2017.
Identifiers: LCCN 2016043892| ISBN 9781138201453 (hardback) |
    ISBN 9781138201460 (pbk.)
Subjects: LCSH: Mathematics—Study and teaching (Elementary)
Classification: LCC QA135.6 .L58 2017 | DDC 372.7—dc23
LC record available at https://lccn.loc.gov/2016043892

ISBN: 978-1-138-20145-3 (hbk)
ISBN: 978-1-138-20146-0 (pbk)
ISBN: 978-1-315-51177-1 (ebk)

Typeset in Palatino
by Apex CoVantage, LLC

To the memories of
Jixuan Liu and Sulan Sun, who instilled in me the love of books,
and to
Zhenglian, my wife, and Isabelle, my daughter.

Contents

Meet the Author

Dr. Fuchang Liu has been an educator for more than three decades, first as an English teacher in China and then as a math teacher in the United States—in this latter role he was named Teacher of the Year in 2002 (he has always been more of a numbers person!). Currently he is associate professor of math education at Wichita State University, working with pre- and in-service elementary teachers on a daily basis.

Dr. Liu's research interests include computational estimation, math anxiety, and mental representations of fractions. He is the author of more than 20 research articles on these topics and coeditor of *Locating Intercultures*, a book on global learning and multicultural understanding. He regularly makes presentations at national and international conferences on issues centering around American children's learning of mathematics.

eResources

The Study Guide found in the Appendix of this book is also available as a free download on our website, so you can easily print and distribute it for meetings. You can access the download by visiting the book product page on our website: www.routledge.com/9781138201460. Then click on the tab that says "eResources," and select the file. It will begin downloading to your computer.

Preface

Jane Smith has been teaching elementary school for a few years now. She loves her children and has been doing a fantastic job teaching them knowledge and skills they'll need for years to come. Nevertheless, like most elementary teachers across the United States, she didn't undergo formal, specialized training in any of the basic subject areas taught in elementary schools: math, language arts, science, and social studies. Rather, her training was elementary education, a major that mainly focuses on methods, the courses that discuss instructional strategies, assessment, and management of those subject areas. Jane has a strong love for the English language and can handle teaching language arts with high proficiency. Science and social studies also come naturally to her. Deep down, though, she sometimes feels a bit unsure about the math topics she teaches. Of course, most of the time she has no difficulty at all. It's just a few minute details that sometimes she's not quite certain about. For example, she's always telling her children that a rectangle has two longer sides and two shorter sides. To her, this feature is what distinguishes a rectangle from a square. But just recently she heard a colleague mention that it wasn't quite correct to explain it that way; that is, the two pairs of sides of a rectangle don't have to be different. Jane knows for certain that a few other teachers in her building teach the same thing concerning rectangles as she does, and now she's not sure if she herself is right or if her colleague is right.

If you are an elementary school teacher like Jane, this book is for you. Written in plain language without using much mathematical jargon, this book examines about 100 common mistakes in teaching elementary school math by analyzing the misunderstanding behind them and then offers advice on how to correct or how not to make them based on the underlying mathematical principles and reasoning.

These mistakes are arranged by topic, such as counting, addition, geometry, and fractions, to name a few, and they're all made by our fictitious teacher Jane Smith. Certainly no one would make this many mistakes, but to make their analysis and discussion easier, this book has to have someone play this bad-guy role. For each mistake, first Jane is quoted as saying something problematic, followed by analysis of what she says, often with the aid of figures or text examples, and then some advice is offered. To help with the flow of the narration, the part about how to avoid making the mistake just discussed is often addressed directly to the reader by using the second person, such as

"You may want to do this or that." Additionally, as the mistakes discussed in this book cover all possible elementary grades, the particular grade level of Jane's children is not specified.

For easy narration, several other fictitious characters are occasionally used in this book. Two of them, Tom and Megan, are children from Jane's class. A Mr. Williams is Jane's colleague, teaching in the room right next to hers.

Despite the book's organization by topic, all chapters—and, in fact, all sections within each chapter—are independent of each other. This meets nicely the needs of the busy, overwhelmed elementary teacher. The reader may read any chapter or section, in any order, without worrying about any other chapter or section. This is particularly useful for the reader at the lesson planning stage when this book may be used as a reference guide.

1

Counting

Counting Shouldn't Start at 0

"Boys and girls, let's have a little practice on counting. Now, count after me. Zero! One! Two! Three! Four!" This is what Jane, the fictitious elementary school teacher in this book, directed her children to do in class one day. On a different occasion, as she found her hundred chart didn't have a 0, she added it there herself, right above the number 10.

While 0 is indeed immediately before 1 in terms of the relative positions for whole numbers, having children count starting at 0 is problematic. Before we embark on further discussion of this issue, let's look at two common kinds of numbers: natural numbers and whole numbers.

Natural numbers are just 1, 2, 3, 4. . . . Why do we call them *natural* numbers? It's because such numbers came into being in the most natural manner. Many things in our lives are considered natural, for example, "natural languages" that came into existence with early human beings, as opposed to "artificial languages" created for a specific purpose. Within natural languages, some phonemes are more natural than others. For example, babies start to pronounce more natural sounds, such as /mɑː/ before less natural sounds such as those containing /r/ or /l/. It's probably not a coincidence that /mɑː/, meaning *mother,* is among the very first few words babies acquire and is found in many languages around the world. Similarly, we can imagine that our ancient ancestors, when the need for numbers started to arise, invented means to represent 1, 2, 3. . . . Henceforth they have become known as natural numbers.

The number 0, in contrast, came into the picture very late. Its concept as used in modern times originated in the 7th century, and this number was introduced into the decimal system as late as in the 13th century (the Roman numeration system, the numerals often used on the face of analog clocks and opening pages of books, still doesn't have a means for expressing 0). This indicates that the representation of 0 is for its "nothingness" instead of counting.

If we add this 0 to the set of natural numbers, then we have whole numbers. That is, natural numbers are 1, 2, 3, 4. . . and whole numbers are 0, 1, 2, 3, 4. . . . Unfortunately, the distinction between *natural numbers* and *whole numbers* is not unanimously agreed on. Sometimes 0 is included in the set of natural numbers. To avoid this confusion, numbers 1, 2, 3, 4. . . have come to acquire a new name: counting numbers.

It may become clear now. Counting numbers, as the term indicates, are numbers used for counting, and they start at 1. If you ask a child who has just learned the first 10 or 20 numbers to count, regardless of the language background that child is from, you will most likely hear "one, two, three, four . . .", not "zero, one, two, three, four . . .".

You may ask, "Are there detrimental consequences for counting starting at zero?"

There are two major problems with counting from 0. First, 0, with its meaning of "nothingness," is very difficult for a young child just learning how to count (believe it or not, even for older children and adults retrieving multiplication facts, the reaction times are longer when a fact contains a 0, such as 3×0, than when a fact doesn't, such as 3×4). Most young children learn their first numbers through a one-to-one correspondence between a number and the quantity of actual objects that number represents, as the number 1 and one toy soldier, the number 2 and two toy soldiers, and so on. Imagine, however, how you would teach a young child to call out 0 with no toy soldiers in sight.

Second, to determine the number of objects by counting, such as determining how many apples there are on the table, many children would touch or point to the first apple and say "one," then move on to the second apple and say "two," and continue in this manner until all the apples are counted (many adults do this too). If we start at 0, we would have to touch nothing and say "zero," but then we would have to start touching apples and calling out "one, two, three," and so on. This can be very confusing because there would be a need to stress when to touch (with a one-to-one correspondence) and when not to touch (without a one-to-one correspondence). If a child accidentally touches an apple while saying "zero," then the total number of apples would be off by 1.

As a matter of fact, you don't even have to look far to see what sequence is actually used in counting. The next time you find yourself counting anything—be it a wad of dollar bills, a group of children, or a number of apples as you put them in a bag when you want to buy 10 at a supermarket—see whether you're saying "one, two, three . . ." or "zero, one, two, three . . .".

What Are Tally Marks for?

To help her children practice counting, Jane did a number of different activities. One of them was to survey her children's favorite types of pizza. She first wrote the few most common types on the board: "Cheese," "Mushroom," and "Pepperoni." Then she asked, "How many of you like cheese pizza best?" Some children raised their hands. Jane led the whole class in counting the number of hands, recorded it with tally marks, and moved on to the next type. After the survey was taken, she had such results on the board (see Figure 1.1).

Jane's use of tally marks, however, was inappropriate for this situation. This is because tally marks aren't nearly as efficient in recording quantities as numbers are. To explore this a little further, let's first take a look at the most common use of tally marks.

Suppose you were doing the same survey, but in a different fashion. After you wrote all the three types of pizza on the board, you asked all your children to go to the board, one by one, and indicate his or her favorite type of pizza under the corresponding label. During this process, numbers would be a poor choice to use. If the first child who preferred pepperoni pizza wrote a 1 under that category, the next child who also liked pepperoni pizza best would have to erase the 1 and write a 2 over it. Similarly, all later children whose favorite type of pizza was pepperoni would erase the previous number and then write a new number over it. This is certainly not an efficient way of recording the survey results. Tally marks, in contrast, fit nicely here. Whoever liked pepperoni pizza best would simply need to put a tally mark under the "Pepperoni" category, and all later children who favored pepperoni would simply need to add another mark under that category. Similarly, those whose favorite pizza was mushroom would simply need to put a tally mark under the "Mushroom" category. No erasing and rewriting would be needed. This is the ideal situation for using tally marks, a situation that requires constantly updating a number.

Figure 1.1 Jane's Survey of Her Children's Favorite Types of Pizza

Cheese	Mushroom	Pepperoni
ɬɬɬ ǁ	ǁǁǁǁ	ɬɬɬ ɬɬɬ ǀ

Tally marks are essentially a one-to-one correspondence between the number of marks and that of actual objects or people (that is, the use of the number of marks representing as many real objects or people). The fact that four marks are drawn in one direction while the fifth is drawn in another is for easy counting at the end of tallying. With every fifth mark traversing the previous four to form a group of five, we can count by 5s instead of by 1s. That should be faster and less prone to error.

But can tally marks be used in place of numbers?

The answer is no. As the name indicates, *tally* marks are just for tallying, and usually for a small number at that. Outside this realm, they are almost useless due to their one-to-one nature, as opposed to the symbolic nature of Arabic numerals such as 4752 (imagine having to represent 4752 using tally marks, not to mention using tally marks to compute). Even for tallying purposes, they are inefficient. Suppose you had a large class and 48 children liked pepperoni pizza best. You would first have to count the tallies to find out. That is why people almost always write down the corresponding total number after tallying a count.

In the aforementioned survey where Jane's children indicated their preferences with a show of hands, the total number for each category was already available when she counted them. She simply needed to write down each number directly. There was no need to draw tally marks. Only when she had to constantly update the number did she need to use tally marks.

It May Not Be Fast—the Purpose of Skip-Counting

"Skip-counting is for counting up to a number faster than counting one by one," Jane told her children one day while teaching the topic of skip-counting. She engaged them in an activity in which they would count out 100 cubes from a pile, first by 1s, then by 2s, and then by 5s. At the end, she showed them the time she had kept so they could see which method got them to 100 the fastest.

First of all, we need to distinguish two types of counting: counting real objects in order to find out their quantity, and counting without any real objects in sight, usually for practicing purposes. Skip-counting is often used in the latter case for understanding the properties of certain numbers in a sequence.

When counting real objects, people may do it by different quantities at a time, such as by 1s, by 2s, and by 5s. You might be tempted to think that as the size to count by increases, the faster it'll be to finish the counting task. This may be true for only a few sizes. Let's suppose we want to count out 100 objects by 1s, 2s, 5s, and 10s to see if some methods are faster than others.

Obviously, counting out objects by 2s is faster than by 1s. Other than that, however, counting by larger numbers probably won't give you an edge, as counting out objects by 5s won't necessarily be faster than by 2s, and counting out objects by 10s won't necessarily be faster than by 5s. The reason is this: Counting objects by 2s doesn't exactly involve counting out two objects sequentially and separately but rather the two objects are counted out at the same time. That is, for two objects, we don't actually count them—we just immediately realize that there're two such objects (this is known as *subitizing*, the perception of a small quantity of 1, 2, or 3 in a very fast manner without actually counting). Therefore, compared with counting by 1s, the number of objects counted out by counting by 2s at each round is doubled ("Two, four, six. . ."). But for numbers 5 and up, the counting can't be skipped. You can easily imagine that counting by 10s won't necessarily be faster than counting by 2s, because for each group of 10, you still need to count them out by a smaller number, such as by 1s or by 2s.

Numbers larger than 10 are rarely used as a group to count real objects by. (Have you ever tried counting real objects by 15s or by 40s?) Still, sometimes it's a good idea to count out objects by a larger number, such as by 5s or by 10s, and leave them in separate piles. The purpose isn't so much for speed as for breaking the whole counting process into several smaller chunks so that if you ever mess up one chunk, you don't have to go all the way back to the beginning and start over again. Instead, all you need to do is recount that particular chunk and go on with the rest of the objects.

The other type of counting—namely, counting without real objects involved—is often used with young children, usually for the purpose of teaching them some sequences of natural numbers and their properties. It's here that skip-counting is used. The following Math in Action box lists the three most common skip-counting sequences. As for skip-counting by 10s, it's not very different from counting by 1s in that we just need to attach a 0 to each number in the sequence of natural numbers: 10, 20, 30 . . . .

> ☑ **Math in Action: The Three Most Common Skip-Counting Sequences**
>
> 1. Skip-counting by 2s starting from 2. This will produce a series of even numbers: 2, 4, 6, 8, ...
> 2. Skip-counting by 2s starting from 1. This will produce a series of odd numbers: 1, 3, 5, 7, ...
> 3. Skip-counting by 5s starting from 5. Such numbers are multiples of 5, and they end in either 5 or 0: 5, 10, 15, 20, ...

Speed in this second type of counting usually isn't a factor to consider. If speed were important, then counting up to 100 could take only two numbers if you counted by 50s: 50, 100. This certainly wouldn't serve any useful purpose at all. Just like counting real objects, numbers larger than 10 aren't often used as a group in counting without using real objects, either. For example, we normally wouldn't ask our children to skip-count by 37s, or by 289s.

Our Number System Is Base-10, Not Base-12

"Boys and girls, let's have a little practice on counting before we learn our lesson today. Now count with me: One! Two! Three! Four! Five! Six! Seven! Eight! Nine! Ten! Eleven! Twelve! Great! Let's start over again." This is how Jane started her lesson one day having her children practice on the first 12 counting numbers.

Counting numbers are 1, 2, 3, 4. . . and they go on and on. For obvious reasons, we don't throw a long sequence of these numbers at young learners all at once. Instead, we introduce such numbers in chunks. We teach them several numbers at one time, then move on to the next several at another time, and this cycle is repeated until they can count up to a fairly large number. Typically, by the time children can count up to 100 and a little bit beyond, most of them can see the pattern in this counting sequence, and teaching them how to count after that isn't quite necessary.

But for the beginning numbers, some consideration needs to be given to how much a chunk should contain. The English number words have some influence on us in this respect, that is, the first 12 words are each completely unique (one, two, three . . . ten, eleven, twelve) and then there is a series of teen-words (thirteen, fourteen, fifteen . . . nineteen). Moreover, there is a special word in English for 12: *dozen*. Reflected in real life, some merchandise is grouped in dozens, such as cartons of eggs and boxes of donuts sold in supermarkets. Due to such influence, Jane used 1 through 12 as the first chunk to teach. However, this isn't ideal. To explore this issue, let's look at the numeration system of the counting numbers we have today.

The numeration system used by most peoples over the world today is the Hindu-Arabic system. This system is what we commonly call the base-10 system, or the decimal system (*deci* means "ten"). In this system, 10 ones form a ten, 10 tens form a hundred, 10 hundreds form a thousand, and so on. In other words, in numbers written out in this system, each place has a value 10 times that of the place to its right. For example, the number 528 means $5 \times 100 + 2 \times 10 + 8 \times 1$. Put in another way, the place held by digit 5 is 10 times that held by digit 2, which in turn is 10 times that held by digit 8.

However, there is a huge obstacle to English-speaking children grasping this concept: the incongruity between Arabic number marks and the corresponding words in English. This is especially true for 2-digit numbers. This issue is reflected in several outstanding aspects. First, the number 11 means 1 ten and 1 one, but the corresponding English word *eleven* doesn't have that indication (at least to people without training in etymology). Similarly, the indication of "two" in *twelve* is too minimal for any child to see.

Second, the English teen-words are in reverse order compared with their corresponding number marks. That is, in "16" the two digits mean 1 ten and 6 ones from left to right, but in the corresponding English word *sixteen*, the part meaning 6 ones is on the left and the part meaning 1 ten is on the right (this is why Jane has often seen her young English-speaking children write "61" when they hear *sixteen*). Moreover, because of this reversion, *sixteen* and *sixty* mean very different things despite their similar lexical structures. *Sixteen* means "six plus ten" whereas *sixty* means "six times ten" (Jane figured out that both *-teen* and *-ty* mean "ten" after she finished her own elementary education).

Third, our numeration system is base-10, and yet the word *ten* appears only once when a child counts from 1 to 100. This delays English-speaking children's understanding that "ten" is a key unit within the base-10 system.

Now, with the English number words posing enough challenges for young learners, Jane was making it a little more difficult when she taught numbers 1 through 12 as a chunk. This further delayed her children's understanding that our numeration system is base-10 and that "ten," as just mentioned, is a key unit within this numeration system.

The way to avoid this problem is to choose the first few chunks based on our base-10 numeration system. As *10* is the key, fundamental unit in this system, it should be treated differently from the other early numbers. Making children pause at 10 is one way of giving it some special treatment. This pause will instill in them the intuition that 1 through 10 is a cycle and after that a new cycle will begin.

If you feel a chunk of 10 numbers is too much to teach at one time, you may want to break it into two smaller chunks: 1 through 5 and then 6 through 10. Two smaller chunks of five numbers each correspond nicely with a human being's two hands of five fingers each. Also, you probably use the ten-frame cards very often at this stage. There is a close correspondence between the two smaller chunks of numbers and the two rows of five dots on a ten-frame card.

2

Number Properties

A Red Marble Isn't More Than a Blue One

After she felt her children had become proficient with 1-digit numbers, Jane wanted to expose them to 2-digit numbers. The first skill she wanted to teach them was how to write 2-digit numbers. She designed two activities to accomplish this task.

Her first activity made use of dominoes. She had Tom, one of her children, come to the front to randomly pick a domino from a box. She then directed him to lay it down horizontally, with the dots facing the whole class. This is what all her children saw (see Figure 2.1):

Jane then drew two short horizontal bars on the board and asked her class, "Now let's look at the domino here. How many dots are there on the

Figure 2.1 The Domino Jane Used to Represent a Supposed 2-Digit Number, 52

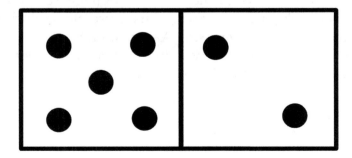

Figure 2.2 Jane's Numeric Representation of the Dots on the Domino

<u>5 2</u>

right? Yes, there are two. And that's our ones digit. It means how many ones we have." She wrote a 2 above the bar on the right. She went on to ask, "How many dots are there on the left? Correct. That's our tens digit. It means how many tens we have." She wrote a 5 above the other bar. Now her number on the board looked as is shown in Figure 2.2, mirroring the dots on the domino.

Since the highest number of dots on either end of a domino is only 6 and Jane wanted her children to be able to write 2-digit numbers with either digit anywhere between 1 and 9 such as 27, 83, or 99, she had her children do another activity. She put nine blue marbles in a jar and nine red marbles in another jar, then put the two jars side by side, with the jar of blue marbles on the right and the one with red marbles on the left (of her children). She said, "Now let's do another activity. When you see blue marbles, their number is just the way you call them. But when you see a red one, it equals ten blue ones. So the blue ones represent our ones digit, and the red ones represent our tens digit." Then she asked Megan to pick some blue and some red marbles, then lay them in front of the jars. Megan picked eight blue and two red marbles. Jane said, "We have eight blue marbles. So that's eight. And we have two red marbles. That's the number of tens. So we have two tens and eight ones. We have twenty-eight altogether."

Both mechanisms for representing 2-digit numbers are somewhat problematic. By how people play dominoes, five dots on the left end of a horizontally laid domino are *not* intrinsically different from five dots on the right end (for a discussion of using playing cards and dice to represent 2-digit numbers, see the next section). Similarly, a red marble is *not* intrinsically 10 times a blue marble: One marble is just one marble, regardless of its color. Simply designating an arbitrary color or one end of a domino as a higher-value number won't help children develop their base-10 and place-value understanding. Instead, it can create much confusion. Jane's children will be forced to regard two single marbles as 20 ones, which runs against their intuitive perception of the objects they see. Consider, for example, an open box containing two red and three blue marbles. Show this box to one of her children after class and ask that child how many marbles there are in the box, and you're likely to hear "five" instead of "twenty-three."

To make the composition of a 2-digit number meaningful to her children, Jane will need to use manipulatives by which a higher-value portion is

Figure 2.3 Base-10 Blocks Are a Great Tool for Representing Multidigit Numbers

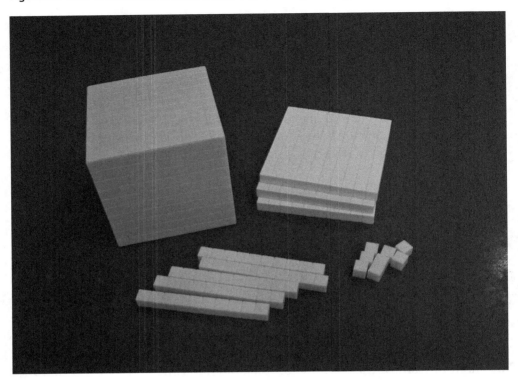

physically and *intrinsically* of a higher value than a lower-value portion. For example, base-10 blocks can do a good job representing ones, tens, hundreds, and thousands (see Figure 2.3). Unit blocks (ones) are each one cubic centimeter in volume, that is, each has a dimension of 1 cm × 1 cm × 1 cm. When 10 such unit cubes are fused together, they become a rod. This rod, representing a 10, is 10 cubic centimeters. Children can see with their own eyes that a rod is made up of 10 unit cubes. In other words, a rod is physically 10 times the unit cube. Similarly, a flat (100) is made up of 10 rods (10 × 10), and a thousand cube (1000) is made up of 10 flats (10 × 100). But usually by the time children start dealing with 3- or 4-digit numbers, their place-value understanding has developed considerably, and flats and thousand cubes aren't as frequently used as unit cubes and rods are.

If Jane represents 28 with 2 rods and 8 unit cubes, her children can make a connection between 2 rods with the 2 at the tens place. This is a good starting point in understanding that the 2 in 28 means 20 (2 tens or rods) instead of 2 single unit cubes (see Figure 2.4). In contrast, two red marbles don't have this property. On the contrary, different colors representing different value

Figure 2.4 The Number 28 Represented by Base-10 Blocks

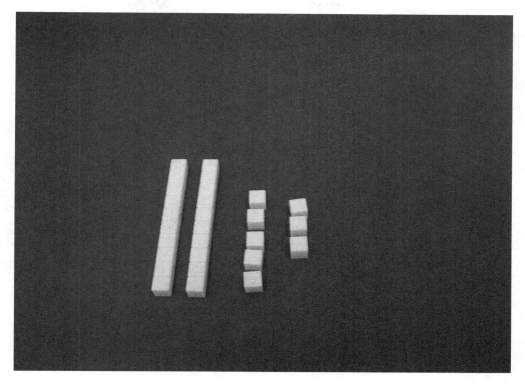

schemes only reinforces the misconception children often have that a double-digit number is simply two single-digit numbers.

Besides base-10 blocks, bundles of sticks are another great tool for representing multidigit numbers. With all sticks being the same size and shape, a bundle can be made by banding 10 single sticks together with a rubber band. Although available commercially, such bundles can be easily made with popsicle sticks, straws, pencils, or some other stick-like objects. Figure 2.5 shows the number 28 represented by bundles made of popsicle sticks, and Figure 2.6 shows the same number represented by bundles made of pencils. Although bundles of sticks and base-10 blocks look rather different, they essentially have the same property: A higher-value unit is physically and intrinsically 10 times its next lower-value unit. Very importantly, children's development of place-value understanding needs to occur when they encounter 2-digit numbers. Even though it's not common to see 10 bundles banded together to form 100, not to mention banding 10 such 100-piece bundles to form 1000, bundles of 10 and some loose ones are usually sufficient in teaching children's understanding of place value.

Figure 2.5 Bundles Made of Popsicle Sticks, Representing the Number 28

Figure 2.6 Bundles Made of Pencils, Representing the Number 28

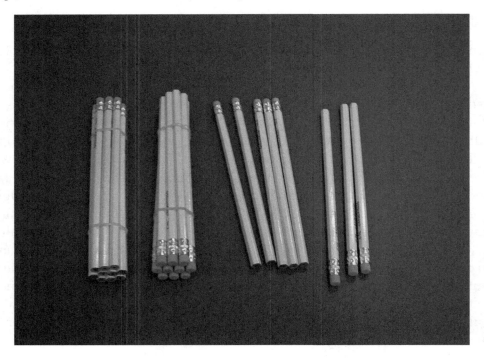

Playing Cards and Dice Aren't Ideal Things to Make Multidigit Numbers With

In engaging her children in a variety of activities and games, Jane often finds herself asking them to make some 2- or even 3-digit numbers. Playing cards are something she frequently uses. She would ask her children to draw one from a deck and lay it down on their desks, then draw another one and put it beside the first one drawn: Now they would have a 2-digit number such as 36. Jane certainly has considered the irregular cards such as aces, jokers, and face cards. She has established the rule that an ace is regarded as a 1, a face card is regarded as a 0, and jokers are not used. So one such number her children made looks like Figure 2.7.

Jane sometimes also uses dice. Because a regular six-sided dice doesn't have digits 7, 8, 9, or 0, she especially likes those 10-sided dice with all 10 digits available. A roll of two such dice can also generate a number like 52 (see Figure 2.8).

Before we discuss the potential problem with using playing cards and dice to make multidigit numbers, let's first take a look at one of the greatest

Figure 2.7 Two Cards Drawn to Make a Supposed 2-Digit Number, 52

Figure 2.8 Two Dice Rolled to Make a Supposed 2-Digit Number, 52

hurdles children face in their learning of elementary math: place value. At the beginning stage, many children have a single-digit concept of multidigit numbers. They often view 2 in 283 just as a 2 instead of 200. Some cultural and linguistic barriers contribute to this difficulty, troubling many children. For example, English number words expressing 2-digit numbers don't explicitly convey the composition of tens and ones (e.g., "twelve" in English as opposed to "ten-two" in some East Asian languages).

Now let's return to the issue of making 2-digit numbers with playing cards. Let's say that Jane handed out a deck of cards to each of her children one day and told them to make a 2-digit number by drawing two cards out of it. Suppose Tom first drew a 5 and then a 2. He might hold one card in his left hand and the other in his right hand. Or he might lay the two cards on his desk with a large space between them. Or he might lay down one card in an up-and-down manner and the other in a left-and-right manner. Or one of the two cards might be red while the other one was black. In all such scenarios, what lies in front of the child doesn't quite look like a 2-digit number.

Using dice may be even worse. Sometimes the two dice rolled may be too far from each other to resemble a 2-digit number, and they may be pointing to opposite directions. On some double dice the digit on the outside is much larger than the one inside it. For a number made with two 10-sided dice, such as the one shown in Figure 2.8, at any given angle one or two other digits are also visible, forming a serious distraction.

Now it is probably easier to see why it's not a good idea to make 2-digit numbers using playing cards or dice. All the situations described here have one thing in common: The 5 and 7 shown on the cards or dice don't quite resemble how a 57 is ordinarily written. They are just two separate, 1-digit numbers. They simply give children the misconception that a 2-digit number is no different from two single-digit numbers. That's certainly not something Jane is wanting to instill in her children.

A way to solve this problem is to make your own cards, with each card showing one bona fide, normally written, 2-digit numbers. When a child draws such a card, it will show 57 just the way it's usually written instead of a 5 and a 7 some distance away or pointing to different directions.

It's Odd Not to Consider 0 as Even

Although not many people will consider 0 as odd, Jane was one of those elementary teachers who sometimes teach children this misconception: 0 is neither odd nor even. This misconception is reflected in the confusion during the oil crisis in the 1970s when some states implemented an odd-even rationing for gasoline, that is, only people with an odd-numbered license plate could purchase gasoline on an odd-numbered day, and only people with an even-numbered license plate could purchase gasoline on an even-numbered day. Story goes that during the first few days of implementing this policy, departments of motor vehicles in those states were flooded with calls from motorists with license plate numbers ending in 0, not knowing whether their numbers were odd or even.

Jane probably got this misconception from the property she had learned that 0 is neither positive nor negative. That property is completely true. For the current issue, however, it's odd not to consider 0 as even. There're several simple things we can do to confirm this.

1. By definition, an integer is even when it is divisible by 2 (that is, it can be evenly divided by 2 with a remainder 0): 0 fits this definition.
2. As we know, odd and even integers alternate on the number line. An odd integer is between two even integers, and likewise, an even integer is between two odd integers. 0 is between two odd integers (−1 and 1).

3. When we count up or down by 2s from an even integer, we will get a sequence of even integers: 0 will be included in this sequence, such as 8, 6, 4, 2, 0 . . . .
4. Using number theory, the following can be proven:
   a) Odd + odd = even, such as 3 + 1 = 4. In 3 + (−3) = 0, 0 fits as an even integer.
   b) Odd + even = odd, such as 3 + 2 = 5. In 3 + 0 = 3, 0 fits in the expression as an even integer.
   c) Even + even = even, such as 4 + 2 = 6. In 4 + 0 = 4, 0 again fits in the expression as an even integer.

Therefore, we can safely conclude that 0 is even.

14 and 37 Don't Belong in the Same List

After discussing multiples, Jane involved her children in a "Butz" game. She put them in a circle. Starting from one child in the circle, all children would take turns to count up, starting from 1. Jane gave these directions: "If anyone is to count a multiple of 7 or a number that contains the digit 7, you call out 'Butz' in place of that number and sit down. Then the person next to you continues. This goes on until only one person remains standing, and that person will be the winner of this game." After a round of the game, Jane asked all those children who had called out "Butz" to recall the number they had to skip. She then wrote all those numbers on the board: 7, 14, 17, 21, 27, 28, 35, 37, ...

This game may have an ill effect on Jane's children's learning of multiples. Simply put, her sequence is actually composed of two different lists mixed together: a list of multiples of 7 (7, 14, 21, 28, 35, and so on) and a list of numbers that contain the digit 7 (7, 17, 27, 37, and so on). These two lists have very little in common and putting them together may confuse children when they need one of them, especially when they need the first. Let's see how.

Suppose Jane's children are now practicing simplifying fractions. Basically, to simplify a fraction means to find a common factor of both the denominator and numerator of the fraction and divide these two numbers by this common factor. If these two numbers have a common factor, it means both of them are multiples of that common factor. For example, $\frac{14}{35}$ can be simplified to $\frac{2}{5}$ because both 14 and 35 have a common factor of 7. In other words, 14 and 35 are multiples of 7.

Now, let's see what happens if Jane gives her children a list of fractions and asks them to simplify them, if possible. One of the fractions is $\frac{14}{37}$. We know 14 and 37 don't have a common factor, and therefore this fraction can't be simplified. However, Jane's children may not think this way. After several days of playing the Butz game, they have gained an inadvertent mastery of that combined list mentioned above: 7, 14, 17, 21, 27, 28, 35, 37, . . . The moment they see this fraction, they would remember that both 14 and 37 are in that "Butz" list and assume that both can be divided by 7. This, of course, is a mistake.

The way to correct this mistake is rather simple: Simply separate the sequence into two lists. As a matter of fact, the list of multiples of 7 may have a wider use in elementary math than the list of numbers containing the digit 7 and therefore should be practiced more. For example, lists of multiples may be used in skip-counting, simplifying fractions, determining if a number is a factor of another number, determining if a number is a multiple of another number, determining if a number is a prime or a composite, and so on.

3

Addition

4 + 4 Isn't Simply 8 Bars Put Together

Jane was teaching "doubles facts," using the example of 4 + 4. She drew four bars on the board, confirmed with her children on that number, and then drew another four bars beside those previously drawn. After that she had her children count the total number of bars she had drawn. Then she wrote out the mathematical expression for the problem: 4 + 4 = 8. Her picture now looked like Figure 3.1.

While Jane's drawing did show the correct answer to 4 + 4, the representation itself was not quite meaningful. First of all, this representation wouldn't help her children make a direct connection with the doubles fact that she wanted them to learn. What they saw was simply a group of 8 bars without being able to see its composition. It's as if she told them the fact without the benefit of a picture at all. Next time they saw 8 bars put together, they probably wouldn't recall the fact she had just taught them. Rather, they might need to count all the bars in order to know the total. Second, what Jane's picture (Figure 3.1) represents is the *result* of 4 + 4, which is 8. Even with whole

Figure 3.1 The 8 Bars Jane Drew to Represent 4 + 4

$$4 + 4 = 8$$

Figure 3.2 An Improved Representation of 4 + 4

$$\mid\mid\mid\mid \quad \mid\mid\mid\mid$$

$$4 + 4 = 8$$

numbers alone, 8 can be the sum of 1 + 7, 2 + 6, 3 + 5, and so on, and Jane's picture doesn't provide a link to the specific components of 4 + 4.

What's more meaningful to a child is a representation that illustrates the *process* as well as the result, not simply the result. Although the process for this particular problem, and for most primary-grade math facts at that, isn't an involved one, still children need to see beneath the surface. To use an analogy, the result part of this problem, 8, is like the upper body of a duck visible above the water surface, whereas the process of the problem is like the duck's feet hidden under the water. Our task is to expose the duck's feet so that children can see it's these feet under the water that drive the duck forward.

To achieve the goal of seeing beneath the surface, Jane will need to demonstrate to her children the process that leads to the final result. For the problem at hand, she should leave a space between the two groups of marks (Figure 3.2) so that her children can make a direct connection between this representation and the doubles fact she wants them to learn. This revised representation will make much more sense because it will help Jane's children recognize that the total number of bars is composed of two equal quantities of 4, and that this total number is 8. If her children, on some other occasion, see two groups of 4 objects each and want to add them together, they can recall this doubles fact and retrieve the answer 8. In other words, the picture in Figure 3.2 represents the two components as well as the result of the problem 4 + 4 = 8, whereas that in Figure 3.1 shows the result part only.

Make Pictorial Representations More Than a "Literal" Translation

After Jane had her children practice on 1-digit addition facts, she moved on to addition of 2-digit numbers. She started with one addend having a value in the lower 10s and made sure that the sum was less than 20. She created this word problem: "There are 12 birds on the tree. 6 more birds come and join them. How many birds are there on the tree in all?" During the problem solving process, Jane drew a picture on the board, with the corresponding mathematical expression for solving the problem under it (see Figure 3.3).

Jane's pictorial representation of this problem was a huge improvement over the one where only the result was given, as shown in Figure 3.1. By

Figure 3.3 Jane's "Literal" Translation of a 2-Digit Addition Problem

$$12 + 6 = 18$$

Figure 3.4 The Quantity of 12 Drawn in Rows of 5

leaving a space between the two groups of birds, the picture for the current problem clearly shows two quantities, 12 and 6, as well as the total number. But there is one problem with it: It seems a bit too "literal." The use of this pictorial representation may be limited when the addends are larger than the few easily perceivable quantities such as 1, 2, and 3 (see *subitizing* discussed on page 5). In this particular example, all the three quantities involved—12, 6, and 18—can't be easily perceived unless her children count them with their fingers. Jane had taught them counting by 5s and using ten-frame cards, but she wasn't taking advantage of these strategies. Rather, she was forcing them to rely on the good old "counting one by one" technique.

Let's see how to represent the same problem in a way that makes better sense to her children. First, let's draw birds in rows of 5, so that the first quantity, 12 birds, will look like Figure 3.4.

This is a much better representation than a row of 12 birds because Jane's children are familiar with the ten-frame card, and the top two rows in this picture match a fully filled ten-frame card perfectly. So they can immediately recognize that those two rows represent 10 birds. With 2 additional birds, they'll easily figure out the quantity involved: 10 + 2 = 12.

Next, let's draw 6 more birds in a different color, or in a different orientation. Let's make sure whenever a row is filled with 5 birds, we move on to the next row. Now, Figure 3.5 is what our new picture looks like.

Along the same line of referring to a ten-frame card, the third and fourth rows in Figure 3.5 also match such a card. With 2 squares on the bottom row

Figure 3.5 The New Quantity of 6 Added, Filling Up Rows of 5

Figure 3.6 The Two Quantities Are Made More Distinct With the Second Quantity Encircled

empty, Jane's children will likely recall that number: 8 (obtained by doing 10 – 2). With 10 birds on the first "ten-frame card" and 8 birds on the second "ten-frame card," the total number becomes obvious: 18.

The technique of counting by 5s can also be used to handle this situation. After Jane draws the two sets of birds together, she may lead her children in counting out by 5s: "five, ten, fifteen!" Then she needs to lead them in counting the three additional ones: "sixteen, seventeen, eighteen!"

Usually a different color for the second quantity of birds would stand out better than the same color with a different orientation. For the picture shown in Figure 3.5, Jane may want to make the second quantity stand out a little more by circling it, as illustrated in Figure 3.6.

In addition to helping children recognize the quantities of 12 or 18 easily, arranging pictorial representations in rows of 5 can help with their later learning as well. Although this is some practice on addition facts, Jane's children have actually also been exposed to some multiplication facts, namely, $1 \times 5 = 5$, $2 \times 5 = 10$, $3 \times 5 = 15$. This is something they will take up soon, and exposing them to such facts will pave the way for handling this later task.

Don't Hop from Square One

As the number line is a very useful tool in handling many math topics, Jane decided to introduce it to her children by using it to model an addition problem. So she drew one on the smartboard, marking a hop to represent 7, and marking another hop to represent 6. Then she wrote the expression represented by this number line: $7 + 6 = 13$ (see Figure 3.7).

But the problem is, the first hop Jane drew covered only 6 spaces, not the 7 she had intended. This mistake would be more obvious if Jane had used addends of a smaller magnitude, such as $3 + 2 = 5$, as shown in Figure 3.8.

Here, the hop representing 3 should be longer than the hop representing 2, as 3 is greater than 2, but in Jane's model the two hops are as long as each other. The correct way of modeling addition problems using the number line is to start the hop at 0, not 1, as shown in Figures 3.9 and 3.10, respectively, for the two problems mentioned here.

Figure 3.7 Jane's Model of $7 + 6 = 13$

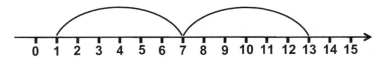

Figure 3.8 Jane's Model of $3 + 2 = 5$

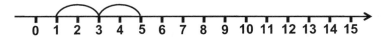

Figure 3.9 The Correct Way of Modeling $7 + 6 = 13$

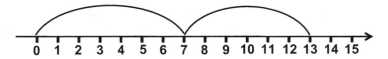

Figure 3.10 The Correct Way of Modeling $3 + 2 = 5$

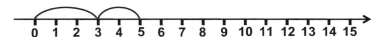

Figure 3.11 The Value of a Number Is the Number of Units It Occupies on the Number Line

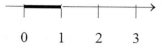

Figure 3.12 A Hop Extends From the Beginning Point to the Ending Point of a Number's Length, or the Number of Units Covered

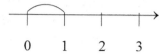

Jane's mistake of starting her first hop at 1 instead of 0 was probably caused by the principle that counting should start at 1, as discussed at the beginning of Chapter 1. These two principles, that counting should start at 1 and that the first hop for an addition problem should start at 0 on the number line, actually don't contradict each other. The perceived incongruity in fact is due to the different mechanisms of representing a number. On the one hand, children's counting at the beginning stage usually involves concrete, discrete objects, such as the number of apples on the table or the number of people in a room. Such numbers can be readily represented by using discrete objects such as counters or blocks. For example, a teacher may use a pile of 7 counters and another pile of 6 counters to model the situation where 7 people in one room and 6 people in another room want to join each other. A number line, on the other hand, isn't composed of a series of separate, discrete points. Rather, it expresses a number's magnitude by specifying its corresponding "length," as can be marked by the number of spaces on this number line. The number 1, for example, occupies 1 space, as shown in Figure 3.11.

If we want to mark this length of 1 with a hop, we have to start the hop at the beginning of this space, which is at 0, and end it at 1, as illustrated in Figure 3.12. If we start the hop at 1, we wouldn't be able to mark off a space of 1 with the endpoint still falling on 1.

Therefore, while counting signifies the node corresponding to the endpoint of a space, drawing a hop on a number line has to cover the whole space, from the beginning point to the endpoint. That's why counting starts at 1 whereas a hop starts at 0.

You Can't Add Apples and Oranges Together

One of Jane's lessons on addition called for teaching her children how to create story problems. For first graders whose writing abilities were quite limited, she wanted to keep such story problems as simple as possible. She came up with a template and wrote it on the board: "I have _____ and _____. How many do I have?" She first created one problem herself, "I have 2 cats and 3 dogs. How many do I have?", which led to her addition problem: $2 + 3 = 5$. She then asked her children to create their own story problems following her template.

But the problem with the story she created immediately became apparent if someone asked her, "How many what?" There may be terms that can describe both cats and dogs such as *pets* or *animals*, but Jane's children can easily make up problems with things of very different categories, such as kites and pencils, toy soldiers and hamsters, picture books and fire engines, or whatever they see or whatever comes to their mind at the moment. Really, none of the pairs just mentioned go together easily. Even with cats and dogs where a higher hierarchical term exists, it may be a difficult task for young children to come up with such a term.

This mistake, of combining things of different categories, actually is not farfetched. A teacher may say, "I need 2 boys to come and stand on this side of our classroom, and I need 3 girls to come and stand on the other side. Now, class, which side has more?" This is the same mistake as Jane made. We can test by asking, "More of what?" A similar example is high school students, when learning how to combine like terms, combining different terms such as $2x + 3x^2 = 5x$ or $2x + 3x^2 = 5x^2$, or worse, $2x + 3x^2 = 5x^3$. When seeing such mistakes, their teachers would often say, "You can't add apples and oranges together. Your x is an apple and your x^2 is an orange. How come you add two apples and three oranges together and get five apples?" or "How come you add two apples and three oranges together and get five oranges?", or, with the previous worst case, "How come you add two apples and three oranges together and get five pears?" Such rhetorical questions drive home the illogicality of adding together things of different categories.

With young children, it is important not to inadvertently give them information with faulty reasoning in it. Although they would not detect the faultiness in their teachers' instruction at this stage, its detrimental effect in the long run can't be overestimated. Many people can remember some faulty information learned at school which troubled the young mind for years to come.

A simple way of fixing this "adding apples and oranges" problem is to use a common category of objects but owned by two different persons: "I have 2 cats. You have 3 cats. How many cats do we have in all?" or "I have 2 dogs. My sister has 3 dogs. How many dogs do my sister and I have?" or "Tom has 2 pencils. Megan has 3 pencils. How many pencils do Tom and Megan have if they put their pencils together?"

4

Subtraction

Don't Make the Kittens Disappear

It was Jane's first lesson on subtraction. She took out 5 counters from a box and laid them out on her desk under the document camera. Then she asked her children: "There are 5 kittens in the room. Now 2 kittens walk away." As she explained the problem, she took 2 counters from among the original 5 and put them back in the box, with 3 remaining on her desk (Figure 4.1). Then she asked, "How many kittens are still in the room?" Her children looked at the remaining counters on her desk and called out, "3!"

Correct. Nevertheless, the purpose of using manipulatives to model a problem isn't just for finding an answer or showing the final result. Rather, it's for demonstrating the *process* of solving a problem. Ultimately, children need to make a connection between the problem being modeled and its representation: 5 − 2 = 3. But the way Jane modeled the problem, as described earlier,

Figure 4.1 Jane's Modeling of 5 − 2 = 3, With Only the Result Visible

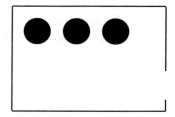

doesn't make it easy for her children to make this connection. The problem solving process appeared to be reduced to a model where not all quantities are visible.

Let's see how we can revise the model a little to stress the problem solving process. The first step is no different from what Jane did, that is, drawing a square representing the room and putting 5 counters in it to represent the original 5 kittens. But when you take 2 counters, representing the 2 kittens that walk away, out of the square, instead of putting them back in the box with the other unused counters, you need to put them outside the square (Figure 4.2). Although the answer is the same, meaning 3 kittens remain in the room, this latter modeling makes it easier for children to see that the total number of kittens is 5 (all those on the desk), the number of those that walk away is 2 (outside the square, but still on the desk), and the number of remaining kittens is 3 (those inside the square). In other words, children can now make a connection with all the three quantities, all visible at the same time, instead of having to keep track of the other two quantities that are no longer present.

Another way of modeling similar problems is to use cards that have a picture on one side and are blank on the other. Explain to your children that a card with the picture side facing up means the kitten is in the room, and when the card is turned over and the picture can't be seen, it means the kitten has walked away. Then Jane's kitten problem may be modeled by laying 5 cards all facing up and telling her children that this means there are 5 kittens in the room. Next, Jane needs to flip over 2 of the cards to indicate that 2 kittens walk away. Now she will want her children to find out how many kittens are still in the room. Her children will likely have an easier time figuring out: 5 (all the cards) − 2 (those flipped over) = 3 (those with pictures still facing up, see Figure 4.3).

Figure 4.2 A Revised Modeling of 5 − 2 = 3, With All Three Quantities Visible

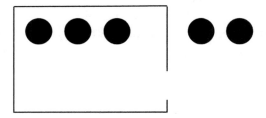

Figure 4.3 A Card Model for 5 − 2 = 3, Where Face-Down Cards Indicate Quantity Subtracted

To sum up, if the kittens disappear as in Jane's original model, children would see only the final result. With the revised model, what children learn is a math fact, $5 - 2 = 3$, with all its components present.

Don't Ever Say "Subtract the Smaller Number from the Larger One"

It's not uncommon, sometimes even for high school students, to confuse a negative number with its positive counterpart. For example, if you ask a class of students "What's $2 - 3$?" you may occasionally hear "1" as well as "-1." Such mistakes can be traced back to as early as first or second grade, when children are learning simple subtraction facts.

This is what Jane did in her classroom one day. She presented a 1-digit subtraction problem, $9 - 4$, to her children and said: "Let's solve this problem. Now subtract the smaller number from the larger number. Tell me your answer."

In subtraction, which number gets subtracted from which number depends on their relative positions. It doesn't have anything to do with their magnitudes. It's a mistake to say "Subtract the smaller number from the larger number," and that can explain why some children may later confuse $3 - 2$ and $2 - 3$.

True, at this stage all facts children learn concerning subtraction are of the type $9 - 4$, that is, the larger number comes first, followed by the smaller one. However, primary-grade children don't stay on this forever. They will, in a matter of a few years, learn $4 - 9$. If they are taught a wrong concept, the detrimental effect may easily carry on to their later learning, sometimes even into high school years.

Let's examine the detrimental effect this mistake may have on children's learning.

First, teaching children to "subtract the smaller number from the larger one" causes them to make a common error like the one exemplified in Figure 4.4, where one can immediately tell that the children are doing exactly what they have been told to do: "Subtract the smaller number from the larger one." This is hardly surprising given that teaching "subtract the smaller

Figure 4.4 When Putting Down a 3 in the Ones Column for This Problem, the Child Is Apparently Trying to "Subtract the Smaller Number From the Larger One"

$$
\begin{array}{r}
36 \\
-19 \\
\hline
3
\end{array}
$$

number from the larger one" on a constant basis will condition children to search for the larger number (or digit in this case) without any regard to that number's relative position.

Second, and more importantly, this "subtract the smaller number from the larger one" rule will instill in children a notion that there's no need to distinguish the two operands in subtraction with regard to their relative positions, in the same way as they apply the commutative property in addition problems (3 + 2 = 2 + 3). But the bad thing about this misconception is that it will become latent without notice, because children at this stage are always given problems in the form of 9 − 4. When they apply the rule of "subtract the smaller number from the larger one," they will always get the correct answer. This, in turn, will reinforce their misconception. They aren't aware that they subtract 4 from 9, not because 9 is greater than 4, but because 9 is before the subtraction sign and 4 is after it. When eventually it's time for them to be exposed to 4 − 9, the misconception, latent for several years by now, will reveal itself. That's why some older children have difficulty distinguishing between 9 − 4 and 4 − 9, and their new teachers will have to work hard to have them unlearn this "subtract the smaller number from the larger one" rule.

Again, in subtraction, which number gets subtracted from which number depends on the operands' relative positions, not their magnitudes. Therefore, don't ever say "subtract the smaller number from the larger number." Instead, for 9 − 4 = , simply say "nine minus four equals . . . ."

"Neither a Borrower nor a Lender Be"—Why We Shouldn't Borrow

Jane learned it that way, and now she's teaching it to her own children: It's the term *borrow* used in solving subtraction problems where the digit in the minuend, the number from which another number is subtracted, is smaller, as shown in Figure 4.5.

Jane described the procedure for solving this problem in this way: "Let's look at the ones column first. We can't subtract 9 from 6, so we go to our next-door neighbor, the tens column, to *borrow* some. This neighbor has enough tens. We *borrow* one from there, so we cross out the 3 and write a 2 above it. Now this one ten we have just *borrowed* becomes 10 ones. Adding the original 6 to this 10, we have 16. Now we can subtract 9 from it. . ."

Figure 4.5 Many People Learned to "Borrow" to Solve This Problem

$$\begin{array}{r} 36 \\ -19 \\ \hline \end{array}$$

So what's wrong with *borrow*?

First of all, when Jane regarded the 6 as being herself and 3 as being her next-door neighbor so that she could borrow from that neighbor, she was treating two components of the same number as two separate, independent entities.[1] This partially contributes to some children' single-digit understanding of multidigit numbers.

Furthermore, in real life, items borrowed should be returned. But we never hear a teacher say, "Now that we are done with our problem, let's return the 10 we have borrowed." This contradiction with real-life experiences can cause children to be doubtful of the math they are learning.

You may ask: What terms should I use in place of *borrow*?

There are several choices.

The most common term is *regroup*, and by far this term is the most widely adopted in elementary math textbooks. *Regrouping* implies that the components of the number are being rearranged so as to execute an operation, such as addition or subtraction. Its use helps prevent a child from having an isolated and unrelated conception of the different parts of the same number.

Another term is *trade*. This term is especially friendly to younger children, as, unlike *regroup*, it is also a term they use in their daily lives. This word captures all the essential connotations *regroup* has. For example, when Megan *trades* her five pennies for a nickel with her mom, the act involves some change of the form of money. The value of the money each party has remains the same.

Two other terms, *compose* and *decompose*, are sometimes used, but they seem to be big words for primary-grade children and, unlike *regroup*, are directional. That is, we usually say "to decompose a ten into 10 ones" and "to compose 10 ones into a ten" but not the other way around.

Can We Subtract a Larger Number from a Smaller One?

When Jane is now teaching subtraction problems such as 36 − 19 where the digit in the minuend is smaller, she would make sure to say *regrouping* in place of *borrowing*. The other parts of her explanation in solving this problem would basically remain the same. This is what she said one day when giving a reason for having to regroup: "Because we can't subtract a larger number from a smaller one, we have to regroup. . . ."

The question boils down to "Can we subtract a larger number from a smaller one?"

The answer is: Yes, we can.

Let's use a real-world situation to explain this. Suppose it's now daytime in Jane's area and the temperature is 35°. The weather forecast says the temperature will drop 20° by midnight. How do we figure out the temperature at midnight? Subtract, for sure. So we do: 35° − 20° = 15°. No big deal. But let's suppose that at a location north of where Jane lives the daytime temperature is also 35°, but because something drastic is occurring there, the weather forecast says the temperature will drop 40° by midnight at that location. What will the new temperature be at midnight? This is an analogous situation and therefore we need to use the same operation, subtraction: 35° − 40°. Now we are truly faced with a situation where we have to subtract a larger number from a smaller one. Would Jane tell her children that there's no way of figuring out the new temperature at that location because "we can't subtract a larger number from a smaller one"?

Let's switch to a similar situation and see whether Jane would be as willing to say "we can't do such and such." In teaching division, Jane would likely start with the simplest case of dividing one 1-digit number by another 1-digit number, with no remainder, such as 6 ÷ 2 = 3 and 8 ÷ 2 = 4. Suppose at this stage a child approaches her and asks, "How do I do 7 ÷ 2?" How would Jane respond? She probably would say, "We haven't learned how to do that yet. But we'll learn that very soon." Or, she might give this child an informal way of solving this problem: "Let's see. You and your sister have 7 apples, and you want to divide them up. Each of you can get 3 apples, and you have one extra remaining. . ." At any rate, Jane would be very unlikely to say, "We can't do that. We can't divide 7 by 2."

Likewise, it's very misleading to tell children that we can't subtract a larger number from a smaller one. It's merely not the time yet for them to learn how to do it.

How do we provide a rationale for learning subtraction requiring regrouping when a digit in the subtrahend is larger than the corresponding one in the minuend, such as 36 − 19? There're several ways to handle this situation. Jane may say, "If the digit in the minuend is smaller, we need to regroup from the tens place. . . ." (For young children, some teachers choose to avoid using the term *minuend* but instead use "the digit on top" when they're referring to a subtraction problem in the vertical setup.) Or, "When the digit in the minuend is not large enough for the digit in the subtrahend, we need to regroup. . . ."

The mathematical content knowledge children learn is a sequence of interrelated topics. They will start with the simplest ones and work their way up to more difficult ones. Some of the topics intended for a later age won't stay out of reach for younger children for long. Sooner or later they'll have to tackle them. Telling them that they can't do a certain type of problem will do them a disservice and create a psychological hurdle that they'll have to overcome later.

10 + 5 − 7 = 15 − 7: No Way to Make It Easier?

Before we take up this topic, let's first make a simple comparison. Of the three subtraction problems listed in the following Math in Action box, which is the easiest? Which is the most difficult?

> **Math in Action: Of the Following Problems, Which Is the Easiest? Which Is the Most Difficult?**
>
> A. 3 − 2 =
> B. 10 − 7 =
> C. 15 − 7 =

Most likely, you will say problem A is the easiest. Both numbers in it are 1-digit and have a low magnitude, and no regrouping is needed in solving it. Problem B is a little more difficult: The magnitude is a little higher, and the minuend (10) is 2-digit. Still, this problem isn't that bad in that even though 10 is 2-digit, it's the very first 2-digit number and a very frequently used benchmark number—all because our numeration system is base-10. When children learn how to add or subtract 1-digit numbers, they easily learn what's known as the make-10 facts, such as 1 + 9 = 10, 2 + 8 = 10, 3 + 7 = 10, and so on.

But problem C, 15 − 7, is very different from the other two: It requires regrouping. Moreover, different people may use quite different strategies to solve it. For example, apart from using direct fact-retrieval, some people may increase 15 by 2 and get 17, then solve two simpler subroutines: first 17 − 7 = 10, and then subtract from 10 the 2 they initially increased 15 by to get 8. Some other people may break 15 into 10 and 5, then use one of the make-10 facts to subtract 7: 10 − 7 = 3, and then add this resulting 3 and the 5 they broke from 15 to get 8. Still other people may break 7 into 5 + 2 so that the original problem now becomes 15 − 5 − 2 = 10 − 2 = 8. The necessity of using several steps in solving such a problem is precisely the reason why subtraction requiring regrouping is difficult and considered a big hurdle for children to overcome after they have learned subtraction with no regrouping.

Having recognized the difficulty involved in subtraction requiring regrouping, let's analyze one problem, 45 − 17, with its vertical setup shown in Figure 4.6, and see if there're ways to make it easier.

The most common procedure for solving this problem is like this: "The 5 in the ones column is smaller than 7, so we need to regroup. We take a 1 in the tens column and the 4 now becomes 3. Then we regroup this 1 ten as 10 ones,

Figure 4.6 The Vertical Setup for 45 − 17

$$
\begin{array}{r}
45 \\
-17 \\
\hline
\end{array}
$$

add the original 5 in the ones column to it, and now we have 15. 15 minus 7 is 8. We write 8 in the ones column. In the tens column, 3 minus 1 is 2, and we write a 2 in the tens column. The result for this problem is 28."

The key step in this procedure is: $10 + 5 − 7 = 15 − 7 = 8$.

As previously mentioned, subtraction requiring regrouping is difficult for children to learn, and here we have a subroutine that requires regrouping. In view of this, a question to ask is, "Is there a way to make this step simpler so that this difficulty may be alleviated?"

You may say, "No way! This is already the simplest we can get. How can there be a simpler way than that?"

Actually the answer is, "Yes, this procedure *can* be made easier."

Let's first review a mathematical property: the associative property of addition. In simple terms, this property states that if you add three numbers (in fact it doesn't matter how many), you will always get the same result regardless of whether you add the first two numbers together first and then add the third number, or whether you add the last two numbers together first and then add the first number. This property can be expressed mathematically as: $(a + b) + c = a + (b + c)$.

This expression is a little misleading in that one will get the impression that there are only two different ways in which two of the three numbers can be chosen and added first. But statistically, with three addends, there should be three ways in which two of them may be added first. That is, a and b may be added first, b and c may be added first, or a and c may be added first. For example, for $1 + 2 + 3$, whichever two numbers you add first, the final result will always be the same. Because a and c are not adjacent to each other in the mathematical expression shown earlier, this third combination is usually skipped.

With this said, $10 + 5 − 7$ can be made easier by doing the third combination first, as shown in the following Math in Action box.

> ☑ **Math in Action: An Easier Way of Solving 10 + 5 − 7**
>
> $10 + 5 − 7$
> $= (10 − 7) + 5$
> $= 3 + 5$
> $= 8$

Figure 4.7 Simplifying Before Multiplying Can Make Solving Such a Problem Much Easier

$$\frac{\overset{1}{\cancel{5}}}{\underset{2}{\cancel{6}}} \times \frac{\overset{1}{\cancel{4}}}{7} \times \frac{\overset{1}{\cancel{3}}}{\underset{\underset{1}{\cancel{5}}}{\cancel{25}}} \times \frac{\overset{3}{\cancel{15}}}{\underset{1}{\cancel{4}}} = \frac{3}{14}$$

Why is this procedure simpler and easier for children? The key reason is that there's no need to regroup. We literally avoid a type C problem as listed at the beginning of this section, and change that into a type B problem by using the associative property. Instead of adding 5 to 10 first to make it a 2-digit number and then having to use regrouping to subtract 7 from it, we subtract 7 from 10 first, using a make-10 fact, and then add 5 to the result. In other words, by subtracting 7 first, we have avoided reaching a 2-digit number and thus avoided having to regroup.

This is a lot like simplifying before multiplying fractions. For example, in solving $\frac{5}{6} \times \frac{4}{7} \times \frac{3}{25} \times \frac{15}{4}$, if we multiply first, our intermediate numbers can end up being very large: $\frac{900}{4200}$. After simplifying these two big numbers, we would get $\frac{3}{14}$. There's a lot of work involved and the procedure is prone to error. For the same problem, if we simplify before multiplying, the whole procedure can be much simpler, because the intermediate numbers never get a chance to become large. Figure 4.7 shows the actual steps.

You may still have doubt about the legitimacy of doing $10 + 5 - 7 = 10 - 7 + 5$, asking, "The associative property is used for addition, but here we have a 'subtract 7' in it. Does it still apply?"

The answer is yes. Addition and subtraction, operationally, are inverse of each other. This means whatever property that applies to addition applies to subtraction, and vice versa, as long as the operation itself is not altered. With regard to the problem at issue, whether we do $10 + 5$ first and then do $- 7$ second or whether we do $10 - 7$ first and then do $+ 5$ second, $- 7$ is still $- 7$ and $+ 5$ is still $+ 5$. Either way the operations themselves are not altered. The only difference is the sequence of these operations, and that is what the associative property is all about.

Note

1 Ma, L. (1999). *Knowing and Teaching Elementary Mathematics: Teachers' Understanding of Fundamental Mathematics in China and the United States.* Mahwah, NJ: Erlbaum.

5

Multiplication

The Formidable 169-Cell Multiplication Table

Jane spent many good hours and finally memorized the multiplication table when she was going to elementary school herself, and now she is teaching the same multiplication table to her own children. After all, people need these multiplication facts on a daily basis and there's every reason for a child to know them by heart. Search on the Internet or in resource books and you'll find this 13 by 13 multiplication table (see Figure 5.1). But that's a total of 169 facts to memorize! That's why during the past several years of teaching this formidable 169-cell multiplication table, Jane resorted to many different strategies. She created some well-rhymed poems, made up some songs, talked to other teachers and found a way of "finger multiplication" for dealing with multiplying by 9, had her children practice skip-counting by 2s and by 5s so that they could memorize the times-2 row and times-5 row easily, and so on. Still, while her children seem to be fine with the first few rows of the table, errors frequently appear when they get to rows of 7, 8, or 9, not to mention the last rows of 11 and 12.

Are there ways to make the multiplication table *itself* simpler? That is, if we keep the multiplication table the way it is, even though we may think of many different strategies to make the memorization process manageable, the total number of the multiplication facts to be memorized is still 169, and this is indeed a daunting task. In contrast, if we can somehow cut down on the total number of facts to be memorized, that will be huge relief for children at this stage.

Figure 5.1 A Common Version of the Multiplication Table, With a Total of 169 Cells

×	0	1	2	3	4	5	6	7	8	9	10	11	12
0	0	0	0	0	0	0	0	0	0	0	0	0	0
1	0	1	2	3	4	5	6	7	8	9	10	11	12
2	0	2	4	6	8	10	12	14	16	18	20	22	24
3	0	3	6	9	12	15	18	21	24	27	30	33	36
4	0	4	8	12	16	20	24	28	32	36	40	44	48
5	0	5	10	15	20	25	30	35	40	45	50	55	60
6	0	6	12	18	24	30	36	42	48	54	60	66	72
7	0	7	14	21	28	35	42	49	56	63	70	77	84
8	0	8	16	24	32	40	48	56	64	72	80	88	96
9	0	9	18	27	36	45	54	63	72	81	90	99	108
10	0	10	20	30	40	50	60	70	80	90	100	110	120
11	0	11	22	33	44	55	66	77	88	99	110	121	132
12	0	12	24	36	48	60	72	84	96	108	120	132	144

You probably have never given it a second thought. "How can it be?" you wonder. "It's been this way forever, and we need all the facts!"

Not really. Let's start by considering several questions here. Did you ever use a multiplication fact containing a 2-digit number, such as 12 × 9, in solving a multiplication problem like the one shown in Figure 5.2? In other words, in solving this problem, even though there is a "12" contained in the first number, did you ever apply "12 × 9 = 108" from the multiplication table? Possibly not. Instead, you most likely took the second number, 9, and multiplied it by 7, then by 2, then by 1, and finally by 8.

The next question is: Why does the multiplication table stop at 12? Why not 13? Why not 18? Why not 47? What is the mathematical reason for including 12 but not 13?

This may have a lot to do with the word *dozen*. As a unit, this word used to be used very often. It's not difficult to envision situations where people

Figure 5.2 Do People Ever Use a Fact Like 12 × 9 = 108 in Solving This Problem?

$$8127$$
$$\underline{\times 9}$$

needed to figure out how many objects there were for, say, seven dozen, and hence the rationale for containing up to 12 in the multiplication table. But if we compare how often people say *dozen* today with how often people used to say it two or three generations ago, we can find that it's not used as often now. In fact, some other non-base-10 units, such as *score* (20) and *gross* (144), are already, to a great extent, out of common use today, and *dozen* may be the very next one to be on the archaic list. This is a natural outcome because the numeration system we use is base-10. It doesn't make much sense to stop in the middle of the second decade of natural numbers.

You may ask, "If we don't stop at 12, what number should we stop at?"

The answer is: Stop at 9. The mathematical reason for this has already been alluded to earlier. For a base-10 numeration system, 0, 1, 2, . . . and 9 are 1-digit numbers. Since numbers beyond 9 are 2-digit, the natural cutoff point is between 9 and 10. No matter how large a number is in a multiplication problem, we handle it one digit at a time (trace your mind to see how you do the problem shown in Figure 5.2). For this reason, no 2-digit number is ever necessary in calculating a multiplication problem. You can safely cross out the last three rows and last three columns from the multiplication table.

Furthermore, if you look at the first row and first column, you will see a series of 0s. Why do we want to subject children to memorizing "0 times 1 is 0, 0 times 2 is 0, 0 times 3 is 0" when we know 0 times whatever number is 0? There's really no need to list all the "0 times. . ." facts in the multiplication table. What children need to know is a simple rule: "0 times any number is 0." Therefore, 0 as a factor can also be taken off the multiplication table and replaced with a simple rule.

Now we have, in effect, eliminated 0, 10, 11, and 12 as factors in the multiplication table. Indeed, factors of 1 through 9, plus a "0 times any number is 0" rule, are sufficient for solving any multiplication problem. That's 81 facts (see Figure 5.3), less than one half the size of the original 169-cell table.

But a table of 81 facts isn't simple enough. Let's take another look at Figure 5.3. If you draw a diagonal line from upper left to lower right through the table (from × to 81) and compare the two halves along this line, you will find that they are symmetrical. Not considering the numbers on this diagonal, every number has a duplicate on the other side of the line. For example, at 6 across and 9 down, there's a 54, and at 9 across and 6 down, there's also a 54. So the next question we need to consider is: Do we really need two sets of numbers, with one set an exact duplicate of the other?

Figure 5.3 A Simplified Version of the Multiplication Table, With 0 and 2-Digit Factors Removed

×	1	2	3	4	5	6	7	8	9
1	1	2	3	4	5	6	7	8	9
2	2	4	6	8	10	12	14	16	18
3	3	6	9	12	15	18	21	24	27
4	4	8	12	16	20	24	28	32	36
5	5	10	15	20	25	30	35	40	45
6	6	12	18	24	30	36	42	48	54
7	7	14	21	28	35	42	49	56	63
8	8	16	24	32	40	48	56	64	72
9	9	18	27	36	45	54	63	72	81

The answer is no. What good does it do to have a table where one part is a mirror image of the other? One set is definitely sufficient.

What, you may ask, if children need to use the other set?

This is where the commutative property comes into play. The commutative property states that in multiplication, if the two factors switch their positions, the resulting product will be exactly the same, namely, $a \times b = b \times a$. Suppose Jane's children have learned that $6 \times 9 = 54$. Let's further suppose that they come across a situation where they need the product of 9×6. By the commutative property, this should have the same result as 6×9 does. What Jane needs to do here is tell her children to safely use the product of 6×9 as the product of 9×6. In other words, we can simply teach children one half of the table. At the same time, we will have to teach them to derive the other half by using the commutative property.

Figure 5.4 A Further Simplified Version of the Multiplication Table, With Only 45 Cells

×	1	2	3	4	5	6	7	8	9
1	1								
2	2	4							
3	3	6	9						
4	4	8	12	16					
5	5	10	15	20	25				
6	6	12	18	24	30	36			
7	7	14	21	28	35	42	49		
8	8	16	24	32	40	48	56	64	
9	9	18	27	36	45	54	63	72	81

Thus, only one section of the original, 169-cell multiplication table is needed. If we draw a right triangle covering 1 through 9, with the hypotenuse running through the square numbers (Figure 5.4), we will have this small section left. But this small section is sufficient for doing *any* multiplication problem. The total number of multiplication facts listed in the new table is a mere 45, about one fourth of the original 169-cell multiplication table.

This 45-cell table can be written out in straightforward mathematical expressions so that children can practice it verbally to memorize it. This written-out table is shown in Figure 5.5.

The multiplication facts as listed in this written-out version are arranged in such a way that the first factor is either smaller than or equal to the second factor. Let's take row 4 for illustration. We start with 1 and multiply this

Figure 5.5 A Written-Out Version of the 45-Cell Multiplication Table

$1 \times 1 = 1$
$1 \times 2 = 2$ $2 \times 2 = 4$
$1 \times 3 = 3$ $2 \times 3 = 6$ $3 \times 3 = 9$
$1 \times 4 = 4$ $2 \times 4 = 8$ $3 \times 4 = 12$ $4 \times 4 = 16$
$1 \times 5 = 5$ $2 \times 5 = 10$ $3 \times 5 = 15$ $4 \times 5 = 20$ $5 \times 5 = 25$
$1 \times 6 = 6$ $2 \times 6 = 12$ $3 \times 6 = 18$ $4 \times 6 = 24$ $5 \times 6 = 30$ $6 \times 6 = 36$
$1 \times 7 = 7$ $2 \times 7 = 14$ $3 \times 7 = 21$ $4 \times 7 = 28$ $5 \times 7 = 35$ $6 \times 7 = 42$ $7 \times 7 = 49$
$1 \times 8 = 8$ $2 \times 8 = 16$ $3 \times 8 = 24$ $4 \times 8 = 32$ $5 \times 8 = 40$ $6 \times 8 = 48$ $7 \times 8 = 56$ $8 \times 8 = 64$
$1 \times 9 = 9$ $2 \times 9 = 18$ $3 \times 9 = 27$ $4 \times 9 = 36$ $5 \times 9 = 45$ $6 \times 9 = 54$ $7 \times 9 = 63$ $8 \times 9 = 72$ $9 \times 9 = 81$

number by 4, and we get $1 \times 4 = 4$. Then we move on to the next number and multiply it by 4, and we get $2 \times 4 = 8$. Next we move on to the next number and get $3 \times 4 = 12$. We then stop at the fact where the two factors are equal to each other: $4 \times 4 = 16$. When we are done with the times-4 row, we move down to the next row (a sequence of numbers times 5).

When children need a multiplication fact where the first factor is smaller than or equal to the second one (such as 5×8 or 8×8), they can retrieve this information directly from the table. When they need a fact where the first factor is larger than the second (such as 8×5), what they need to do is simply switch the positions of the two factors and come up with the product.

"You Must Put a Zero in the Ones Place"

In doing multidigit multiplication problems, Jane's children often make the mistake of treating a 2-digit number as two separate, 1-digit numbers. For example, Tom did a 2-digit by 2-digit multiplication problem as shown in Figure 5.6.

Since this is a very common mistake among elementary school children, Jane said to her class, "When you come down to the second row, you *must* put a zero in the ones place and then put your numbers next to it." She showed her children her way of doing this problem (see Figure 5.7).

Some other times Jane stressed her point by writing the 0 in a different color, or writing some other symbols such as a $\times$, *, or even drawing a simple figure such as an apple. By having her children put a 0 (or some other symbols, for that matter) in the ones place, she has effectively forced her children to start writing their ones column over to the left. But is such a 0 a *must* in this case?

Not really. Many people actually do this problem in a "staircase" format and still get the correct answer (see Figure 5.8).

Figure 5.6 A Common Mistake in Doing Multidigit Multiplication Problems

$$
\begin{array}{r}
43 \\
\times 57 \\
\hline
301 \\
215 \\
\hline
516
\end{array}
$$

Figure 5.7 Jane's Way of Doing This Problem, by Using a 0

$$
\begin{array}{r}
43 \\
\times 57 \\
\hline
301 \\
2150 \\
\hline
2451
\end{array}
$$

Figure 5.8 The "Staircase" Format in Doing This Problem

$$
\begin{array}{r}
43 \\
\times 57 \\
\hline
301 \\
215 \\
\hline
2451
\end{array}
$$

Apparently, this last setup indicates that a 0 in the ones place is not mandatory. To help children understand why they make the mistake as Tom did, Jane needs to ask herself this question: What's the rationale for putting a 0 in the ones place? After this question is answered, whether or not to put a 0 in the ones place will become a minor issue.

In order to see the reason behind putting a 0 in the ones place, we need to delve deeper into a learner's thinking as to how they make such mistakes. Many children during elementary school years have a 1-digit understanding of multidigit numbers. For the current problem, Tom first took 7 and multiplied it with 43. But problem occurred when he moved on to the next column: He treated the 5 in 57 as 5 ones. He retrieved all multiplication facts correctly, added the two rows correctly, but failed to understand that the 5 in 57 means 50, or 5 tens.

If we write 57 in its expanded form, then the problem at hand will become clearer: $57 = 50 + 7$, therefore $43 \times 57 = 43 \times (50 + 7)$. By the distributive property, $43 \times (50 + 7) = 43 \times 50 + 43 \times 7$. Tom did the 43×7 part correctly, but not the 43×50 part. Since he treated the 5 in 57 as 5 ones, he got $43 \times 5 = 215$ ones. In fact, the final result he got, 516, is exactly $43 \times (5 + 7) = 43 \times 12$. This just shows that Tom, in the process of doing this 2-digit by 2-digit problem, treated 57 as a 5 and a 7 put together instead of treating it as composed of 5 tens and 7 ones.

Realizing the nature of such mistakes, Jane can specify the procedure by either "putting a zero in the ones column" or "starting the tens digit in the tens column." If she wants to go by "putting a zero in the ones column," she may want to avoid saying *must*. This method of using a 0 in the ones place is only procedurally forcing children not to write anything there. In contrast, if she wants to go by "starting the second row in the tens column," Jane may want to give some explanation along this line: "The 5 in 57 is in the tens place, so it is 5 tens. Now 3 times 5 tens is 15 tens, so we need to write this number as tens. Now we put down a 5 in the tens column . . . ."

Can You Move over One Place Value?

While teaching multiplying two double-digit numbers, Jane soon found that the mistake her children were making—of not lining up the numbers correctly—was a frequent one (see Figure 5.6). After some contemplation, Jane felt that she needed to take up the notion of place value. In correcting the mistake exemplified in the problem discussed earlier, she said, "You must keep your numbers in the appropriate place value. After you're done multiplying the first digit, 7, you must move over one place value to the left and write your results directly under the tens digit, 5, ..."

The question is: Can she "move over one place value"? To see the problem with Jane's use of *place value*, we need to look at what place value is.

What is place value? Precisely as the term indicates, place value refers to the fact that each place in an Arabic number has an assigned value. Specifically, in the Hindu-Arabic numeration system, the values of the digits of a number are, starting from the right side to the left, 1, 10, 100, 1000, and so on. That's why we say ones place, tens place, hundreds place, and so on. For example, in 435, 5 is in the ones place, or we may say that 5 has a place value of ones. Over to the left, 3 has a value of tens and 4 has a value of hundreds. To get the magnitude of this number, we have to multiply each digit by its place value and then add up the partial products. The total value of 435, therefore, is, if we list largest values first: $4 \times 100 + 3 \times 10 + 5 \times 1$. This, by the way, is called the expanded form of 435.

Thus, place value is a "value." It is not something like a spot or something people can move about. It's as if we have marked a "price" for each place within a number. In the aforementioned number 435, it's as if 5 was carrying a price tag of $1, and it was yelling, "The price for us is $1 each. There are five of us, and we are worth $5." Similarly, it's as if 3 was saying, "The price for us is $10 each. There are three of us, and we are worth $30," and 4 was saying, "The price for us is $100 each, and we are worth $400." While people can move price tags to be put on different items, they can't physically move a price. A price is a value or feature assigned to a merchandise.

Back to what Jane said that her children "must move one place value to the left," she confused *place value* with *place* or *column*. The following Math in Action box lists some incorrect or improper uses of the term *place value:* In each case, it should be replaced with either *place* or *column*.

> ☑ **Math in Action: Incorrect Ways of Using *Place Value***
>
> - You should put your digit in the right place value.
> - You lined up your place values wrong.
> - You need to move the next partial product over one place value.
> - The mistake you made was misplacement of the place value.
> - You should shift your numbers to the left one place value.

Line Multiplication: Why It Doesn't Work

Jane heard of a new method of multiplication, line multiplication, from Mr. Williams, the teacher in the room next door to hers. Mr. Williams mentioned that the good thing about this method is that children don't even have to memorize any multiplication facts: All they have to know is how to count. Jane got curious and had him demonstrate the procedure to her in great detail after school one day so as to assess the feasibility of teaching it to her own children. This is how Mr. Williams told her how it works: "Suppose you want to do 12 × 31. You first draw one line, representing the tens digit, leave some space, and then draw two lines, representing the ones place for the first factor, 12, with all the lines tilting up on the right (see Figure 5.9a). Next, you draw lines for the second factor in a similar fashion, over the first factor drawn, but tilting down on the right. Now you have two sets of lines crossing each other, forming four groups of crosses (see Figure 5.9b)."

"Now here's the easy part," Mr. Williams continued. "You just circle the crosses from left to right and count them. The circle on the left has three crosses in it, and you write a 3 under it. The one in the middle has two groups of crosses, but count them together, and there are seven. Write a 7 under the middle circle. The one on the right has two crosses in it, and write a 2 under it. Now your final answer is 372" (see Figure 5.9c). After a pause, he continued, "You see, you don't need to know a single multiplication fact with this method."

Figure 5.9 Line Multiplication Showing 12 × 31.

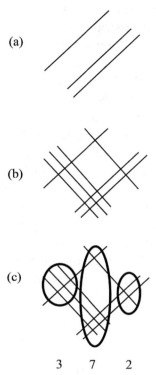

(a)

(b)

(c)

3   7   2

(a) Lines representing 12; (b) Lines slanting the other way, representing 31, drawn over the previously drawn 12; (c) three groups of intersections indicating the product of 372

Jane was impressed. In fact, she thought this method was so cool that she decided to teach it to her own children. After all, when this could be used without having to use a single multiplication fact, why bother with the traditional method, which requires a good amount of time spent on having children memorize the multiplication table?

However, except for a limited number of situations, this method won't work. It has some serious flaws that shouldn't be overlooked.

First of all, the multiplication facts, or the whole multiplication table, are there for an obvious reason: We don't want to count the total number of elements every single time when they are in groups with each group having an equal number of elements in it: for example, counting 5 rows of 8 chairs each. For this situation, we don't even want to use repeated addition to obtain the total every single time (8 + 8 + 8 + 8 + 8 = 40). Instead, a single multiplication fact will take care of it (5 × 8 = 40). Line multiplication is dragging children back to, not repeated addition, but counting.

Second, drawing lines and then counting the crosses can be time consuming. This is especially true if the digits involved have a higher magnitude. Imagine multiplying 789 × 987 using this method. Before a child even finishes drawing all the 48 lines (they take up a lot of space, too), another child using the traditional method could very well finish the whole problem. In other words, this method can handle numbers composed of lower-magnitude digits such as 1, 2, and 3 at best. That is probably why Mr. Williams showed Jane a problem with lower-magnitude digits only.

Third, if a problem takes more time to do, then usually it's more prone to error. A simple calculation reveals that when doing 789 × 987 using line multiplication, there will be more than 500 crosses to count! A child has to be very attentive to not make any errors in this long process.

Fourth, when there're more and more digits in a factor, then this method will become more and more clumsy, to the point it's practically impossible to handle. Imagine yourself doing a 4-digit by 4-digit problem using this method. It's difficult even without using digits of higher magnitude.

For these reasons, stay clear of this line multiplication.

6

Division

The Larger Number Doesn't Always Go Inside

After she introduced division and the long division symbol, Jane presented to her children a problem for demonstration: 8 ÷ 4. She explained the procedure in this way: "You first draw this symbol for long division ($\overline{)}$). Then you put the larger number inside this symbol. Next, you put the smaller number outside. . . ."

True, at the beginning stage of learning division, children are only exposed to problems such as the one just mentioned, where the dividend (the number to be divided) is larger than the divisor. That's because they won't be able to properly handle a problem where the dividend is smaller than the divisor before they learn decimals and fractions. However, in a mathematical expression for division, which operand gets divided by which operand doesn't depend on their magnitudes. Instead, each operand's relative position determines whether it's the number to be divided, or the one to be divided by. This is very much like the previously discussed subtraction problem where which operand is subtracted from which operand doesn't depend on their magnitudes but rather their relative positions.

Saying "the larger number goes inside" can cause serious misunderstanding on children's part. Naturally, after they have heard this "larger number goes inside" procedure a sufficient number of times, their minds are conditioned to the magnitude of each operand when they see a division problem. Later, when they do have to deal with 4 ÷ 8, some of them would automatically put the larger operand, 8 in this case, inside the long division symbol. Of course, this will cause them to produce a wrong answer. Moreover, by the time they learn decimals, their wrong impression will be so deep-rooted that they'll have difficulty distinguishing between $8 \div 4$ and $4 \div 8$.

The proper way of handling this situation is simply to identify the *position* of each operand. For $8 \div 4$, say, "Put the number before the division sign inside the long division symbol," or, "Put the first number inside the long division symbol." That is, $8 \div 4$ is set up as $4\overline{)8}$. Later, when you teach decimals, you'll find yourself saying the same thing for $4 \div 8$: "Put the number before the division sign inside the long division symbol," and the setup will be $8\overline{)4}$. In each case, the meaning of the division is maintained, and you don't need to worry about how to change children's habit of identifying the larger operand to that of identifying the first operand in a division sentence. The relationship between the dividend and divisor should be kept consistent.

What's 0 ÷ 0?

Jane learned, from all the math courses she had taken, that she cannot divide by 0. Anyway, for a long division problem as shown in Figure 6.1, what number can go in the quotient's spot (indicated by a question mark) such that $0 \times ? = 8$? No number will ever work, because 0 times any number is 0.

Jane is fine with this "cannot divide by 0" rule. But the next problem gives her a lot of trouble: What's $0 \div 0$?

At first Jane thought the answer was 0. She reasoned this way: "We don't have anything to start with, and then we divide this nothing by nothing. What else can the answer be except zero?" Jane even came up with the long division setup (see Figure 6.2) to support her choice.

Figure 6.1 For This Problem, no Number Fits Where "?" Is Displayed Such That $0 \times ? = 8$

$$
\begin{array}{r}
? \\
0\overline{)\,8} \\
\underline{8} \\
0
\end{array}
$$

Figure 6.2 Jane Set Up 0 ÷ 0 in This Way to Show That the Result Is 0

$$
\begin{array}{r}
0 \\
0\overline{)\,0} \\
\underline{-\,0} \\
0
\end{array}
$$

Figure 6.3 It Seems a 5 Will Work in Jane's Setup

$$
\begin{array}{r}
5 \\
0 \overline{\smash{)}\ 0} \\
-\,0 \\
\hline
0
\end{array}
$$

Jane discussed this with Mr. Williams and was surprised to learn that he thought the answer was 1. He said, "When a number is divided by itself, the result is 1. For example, $25 \div 25 = 1$, $3.78 \div 3.78 = 1$, and so on. By the same rule, $0 \div 0 = 1$."

Unfortunately, neither Jane nor Mr. Williams was correct.

Since the mistake of saying $0 \div 0 = 0$ is very common, we need to give it a thorough examination.

Let's first use Jane's setup (shown in Figure 6.2) and see whether it'll work if we replace Jane's original 0 with a 5 (see Figure 6.3). It seems it does, as 0 times 5 *is* 0. But if we extend the same line of thought from here, it appears any number can go in that spot, as 0 times any number is 0. So what's $0 \div 0$? 0? 5? 12? 0.009? The list can go on and on, and Jane isn't so sure now.

Actually, having many possible answers is exactly the reason why $0 \div 0$ is *not* 0. When a problem has one possible answer, say $3 + 2$, that problem is said to be *defined*. This isn't, however, the case with $0 \div 0$. We have just seen that infinitely many numbers can go in the quotient's spot in Jane's long division setup. When such is the case, it's said to be *undefined*.

For emphasis, *$0 \div 0$ is undefined.* This is consistent with the general rule: We cannot divide by 0.

You may want to check this out on a calculator. Punch in $0 \div 0$ on a calculator and it will display a message such as "Error," "Dividing-By-0 Error," or "Undefined." For this matter, even the most primitive calculator will produce an error message.

"Is there a real-world situation," you may ask, "which you can use to illustrate your point, that is, $0 \div 0$ won't produce a meaningful result?"

Certainly. Let's suppose you're watching a women's basketball game and the players' free-throw percentages for that particular game are displayed on television. In order to calculate a player's free-throw percentage, all we need to do is divide the number of free throws made by the total number of free-throws attempted. Suppose player A has had 10 free throw chances and made 9 baskets. Her free-throw percentage for this game is $9 \div 10 = 90\%$. Let's further suppose player B also has had 10 chances but made 4 baskets. Her free-throw percentage is $4 \div 10 = 40\%$. Now let's look at player C. This player hasn't been fouled at all during the game and hasn't been awarded any free-throw chances (0 attempts). Of course, when she hasn't had any free-throw

Figure 6.4 The Rule About a Number Divided by Itself Being 1: It Works for Any Number But 0

$$\frac{n}{n} = 1 \ (n \neq 0)$$

chances, she has made no baskets in this regard. In order to calculate her free-throw percentage, we need to apply the same formula: Divide the number of free throws made by the total number of free throws attempted, and in this case, it's 0 ÷ 0. So what's player C's free-throw percentage—0%? If she's good at making free throws, she would certainly protest and say, "If I'd got some chances, I sure would have made some baskets. How come I got 0% here?" She really has a point.

Then 0 ÷ 0 = 100% (which equals 1)? This doesn't make sense either. If that player turns out to be a poor free-throw shooter, people would wonder, "She's not a particularly good free-throw shooter, and now she got a perfect free-throw percentage?"

In all likelihood, your television screen won't display a percentage for player C. The best description may just be "0 of 0" (0 baskets made, of 0 attempts). No actual percentage whatsoever fits in this situation.

The lesson to draw from this mistake is: Under no circumstances should a person attempt to divide *any* number by 0. In other words, even if this number is 0, still you may not divide it by 0.

Back to Mr. William's reasoning: If he wants to formulate a rule concerning a number divided by itself, it should be expressed as in Figure 6.4, in a rigorous manner, with a condition attached that 0 shouldn't be used as the divisor.

Division Isn't Always Repeated Subtraction

Let's say Jane wanted to demonstrate to her children how to divide 21 cards evenly among 3 children. Using 21 counters representing 21 cards, Jane took 7 out from the pile and put them on a separate spot, saying, "Tom will get 7 cards. Let's put them here for Tom." She then took another 7 out and said, "Now there are 7 cards for Megan. Let's put them here for her." She went over the process again for the third child. Her children could see there were 7 counters for each of the 3 children. But is this a correct way for modeling this problem?

The answer is no. But the error isn't easy to see because all the numbers used (21 and 3) are small and the multiplication fact involved (3 × 7 = 21) is well known to everyone. So let's choose a different set of numbers and see if we can still do the problem the same way as Jane divided 21 cards among 3 children.

Let's suppose we want to divide 442 cards among 17 children. How many cards should we take out for child A? Most of us wouldn't have a ready answer for 17 × __ = 442, and therefore we wouldn't have any idea about the right number of cards to take out for child A.

Now the problem with Jane taking out 7 cards for Tom is clear. Jane did that because she already knew the answer (7) before she started doing the problem. But actually that was exactly the number she was trying to figure out! Why did she need to go through all the trouble when she already knew it was 7?

When the numbers involved are larger (such as 442 and 17) and the answer is not apparent, we can't take out a certain number of cards for child A, then take out the same number of cards for child B, and so on, because we don't know the exact number of cards to take out for each child. This is because there are two different interpretations for division, depending on which factor in the corresponding multiplication problem we are trying to figure out. For a multiplication problem such as "There are 4 bags of apples. Each bag contains 6 apples. How many apples are there in all?", we normally use the first factor to represent the number of groups and the second factor to represent the number of elements in each group (4 × 6). If the number of groups is unknown (such as "How many bags will be needed to pack up 24 apples if each bag can contain 6?", transcribed as 24 ÷ 6 = ?), the interpretation for this division problem is called *subtractive*. The person who does the packing can repeatedly take 6 apples out of a pile of 24 and put them in a bag until the pile is finished with. Then, if the number of elements is unknown ("Jane has 21 cards and wants to divide them up among her 3 children. How many cards will each child get?"), the interpretation for this division problem is called *distributive*—Jane has to give one card to each of her 3 children (to distribute). If the remaining cards are sufficient to go another round, Jane has to continue with the process, that is, give one card to each child, until there are no more cards left or until the number of cards left is not enough to go another round. This is exactly the problem presented at the beginning of this section, one involving the distributive interpretation.

In summary, there are two interpretations of division, subtractive and distributive. The common saying "Division is repeated subtraction" is applicable to the subtractive interpretation but not to the distributive interpretation—and the modeling for one interpretation is different from that for the other. When modeling the subtractive interpretation such as "How many bags will be needed to pack up 24 apples if each bag can contain 6?", you repeatedly take out groups of 6. But when modeling the distributive interpretation, such as "Jane has 21 cards and wants to divide them up among her 3 children," you have to distribute one card to each child and repeat the process until it's over, rather than take out 7 and give them to one child. In other words, you don't know each child will get 7 before you finish the process.

"Dad, Mom, Sister, Brother, Rover": Where Is Dad?

Jane presented to her children the procedure for long division of a 2-digit number by a 1-digit number, as shown in Figure 6.5.

To help her children remember the order of carrying out the steps involved in long division, Jane taught them a mnemonic she heard from Mr. Williams: "Dad, Mom, Sister, Brother, and Rover," where the first letters stand for "Divide, Multiply, Subtract, Bring Down, and Repeat."

Here is a problem, though. For the very first step, "divide," what exactly are children supposed to do before they take on the second step, "multiply"? For the example shown in Figure 6.5, what should occur before Jane's children do 1 × 4?

With this saying, Jane made two logical errors that can be confusing to her children. First, isn't the whole thing Jane was teaching called "division"? That is, to divide 56 by 4, we need to divide, multiply, subtract, bring down, and so on. When the whole thing is "divide," and this first step of the process is also "divide," then what's the relationship between them? Second, "divide" has no specific action tied to it as the other verbs do. It seems this action is fused with the second verb, "multiply." Children may wonder, "What exactly should I do for dividing?"

The rationale for creating such a saying to help children remember the order of carrying out the steps involved in doing a long division problem isn't a strong one. This is not like solving a problem involving the order of operations, such as 4 + 5 × 3, where 5 × 3 must be carried out first. Without knowing the correct order of operations, children most likely would solve this problem from left to right, resulting in a wrong answer—hence a rationale for verbalizing the order of operations ("multiplication/division before addition/subtraction") in

Figure 6.5 A Long Division Problem Jane Used for Demonstrating "Dad, Mom, Sister, Brother, and Rover"

$$
\begin{array}{r}
14 \\
4{\overline{\smash{\big)}\,56}} \\
\underline{4} \\
16 \\
\underline{16} \\
0
\end{array}
$$

a way that can help children best memorize it. However, in solving a division problem such as the one in Figure 6.5, there are various hints suggesting what to do next. For example, it is not even possible for children to do the "bring down" step at the very beginning. Similarly, they probably wouldn't subtract before the "multiply" step, as there is no number to subtract yet.

In short, this mnemonic is a little farfetched and not quite necessary.

Division Doesn't Always Yield a Smaller Number

When Jane teaches a certain math topic, she almost always wants to make it related to other math topics such that her children can easily see the interconnection among them. It's no different when she brought up division. While teaching this topic, Jane said, "We learned multiplication, which we use to make numbers larger. What we are going to learn today is the opposite operation, an operation we use to make numbers smaller. This is division."

Certainly when children first learn multiplication and division, the problems they encounter consist of positive integers only. If we multiply one positive integer, say, 4, by another positive integer, say, 2, we will get an integer larger than either of the two others, as shown in the following Math in Action box.

Math in Action: Multiplication Problems in which We Get Larger Numbers

$4 \times 2 = 8$
$8 \times 2 = 16$
$16 \times 2 = 32$
. . .

Likewise, when we divide a positive integer by another, this integer will often become smaller, such as the examples shown in the following Math in Action box.

Math in Action: In These Division Problems, the Results Are Getting Smaller and Smaller

$64 \div 2 = 32$
$32 \div 2 = 16$
$16 \div 2 = 8$
. . .

However, children will soon learn fractions and decimals—and once they do, they will find what their teachers have said concerning multiplication yielding larger results and division yielding smaller results to be incorrect. Let's create two story problems, presented in the following Math in Action boxes, to demonstrate this point.

☑ **Math in Action: A Story Problem where Multiplication Yields a Smaller Number**

At the pizza party for his 18 children, Mr. Williams gave each child one half of a pizza. How many whole pizzas did Mr. Williams give out to his children?

We certainly need to use multiplication to solve this problem: $18 \times \frac{1}{2} = 9$.

After multiplying, instead of larger number, we get a smaller one.

Additionally, if we multiply a number by 1, we don't get a larger result either: We get an identical number back, such as $4 \times 1 = 4$ (that's why this property is known as the multiplicative *identity* property).

Similarly, division can yield a larger result than what children start with. The following Math in Action box presents one such story problem.

☑ **Math in Action: A Story Problem where Division Yields a Larger Result**

Mr. Williams wants to make some cakes to entertain his children. The recipe calls for 0.2 kg of flour per cake. Mr. Williams has 4 kg of flour. How many cakes can he make?

Here, we need to use division to solve this problem: $4 \div 0.2 = 20$.

Similar with multiplication, division by 1 will not produce a smaller number, either. Instead, it produces an identical result, such as $4 \div 1 = 4$.

To sum up, Jane's statement about multiplication yielding a larger number and division yielding a smaller number is true only if the multiplier or divisor is greater than 1 (see the multiplying and dividing by 2 problems shown in the first and second Math in Action boxes). If the multiplier is less than 1 and greater than 0, then multiplication will yield a smaller number, as in the pizza example. In a similar manner, if the divisor is less than 1 but greater than 0, then division will yield a larger number, as in the cake example. Additionally, multiplication and division can yield an identical result by multiplying or dividing by 1.

Although we did not discuss this error when we were talking about addition and subtraction, it's a similar mistake to say "Addition will always give you a larger number" and "Subtraction will always give you a smaller number." These statements are true only if the numbers to be added or subtracted are positive. If we use negative numbers or zeros, we can easily come up with counterexamples to these generalizations, as listed in the following Math in Action box.

 Math in Action: Counterexamples of "Addition always Yields Larger Numbers", and "Subtraction always Yields Smaller Numbers"

$8 + (-3) = 5$
$8 + 0 = 8$
$8 - (-3) = 11$
$8 - 0 = 8$

Thus, we should be very careful about making generalizations. What seems to be true at the current time may not necessarily be so in a few years. Vice versa, what does not seem to be true at the current time may soon be something children will be focusing on intensively.

7

The Order of Operations

Aunt Sally Is Evil—The Order of Operations

After her children had learned all the four basic operations—addition, subtraction, multiplication, and division—and been exposed to parentheses and exponents, it was time for Jane to teach them the order of operations. Jane had learned a mnemonic when she was going to elementary school herself, and now she was about to teach the same thing to her own children. After all, about all the teachers around her were teaching the same thing, and all their children could say it fluently. So what else would she do to teach the order of operations? Jane did not even give it a second thought when she passed this mnemonic on to her children: "Please Excuse My Dear Aunt Sally," PEMDAS for short, which stands for *parenthesis, exponent, multiplication, division, addition*, and *subtraction*. For one of the problems Jane gave for exercise, $7 - 2 + 3$, her children applied the rule by doing $2 + 3$ first, with a resulting 5, and then doing $7 - 5$. The final answer every child got was 2.

But the right answer is *not* 2.

Nothing is more misleading than this mnemonic in teaching elementary school math. In fact, it has been, and still is, causing tens of thousands of children to make mistakes on a problem as simple as $7 - 2 + 3$.

The first person who came up with this mnemonic no doubt meant well. Obviously it was created to help children memorize the order of operations for a problem having two or more operations in it. But if we look at the receiving end, it may be a totally different picture. When elementary school children are presented with the order of operations in a linear, sequential manner as PEMDAS, they will naturally interpret it as meaning that any operation takes precedence over those following it. More specifically, children interpret PEMDAS as meaning that multiplication comes before division and that addition comes before subtraction, because the mnemonic says "M-D-A-S".

In actual fact, the rule regarding the order of operations states that addition and subtraction are on the same level and should be carried out from left to right. Neither operation has precedence over the other. Thus, for doing the problem at issue, the correct procedure is: $7 - 2 + 3 = 5 + 3 = 8$. And the same is true for multiplication and division. These two operations are on the same level and should be performed from left to right. For example, for $18 \div 3 \times 2$, the right procedure is $18 \div 3 \times 2 = 6 \times 2 = 12$.

You may be puzzled now, because you have, just as Jane has, been doing $7 - 2 + 3 = 7 - 5 = 2$ and $18 \div 3 \times 2 = 18 \div 6 = 3$ all your life. After all, who would doubt the widespread mnemonic "Please Excuse My Dear Aunt Sally," which many elementary teachers say year after year, in the first place? But being widespread doesn't necessarily mean being correct, and this particular mnemonic clearly is not. In fact, it's harmed much more than helped children learning the order of operations.

Let's take a moment to see why $7 - 2 + 3$ *can't* equal 2. Let's use two different methods to analyze it.

We can first use proof by contradiction to handle this problem. To start, let's assume $7 - 2 + 3 = 2$ is true; if it leads to a contradiction, then we conclude that it's false. Next, let's use a different problem of a similar structure: $7 - 2 - 3$. Nobody will have any problem in coming up with the correct answer: $7 - 2 - 3 = 2$. Since both problems have the same answer, it must follow that $7 - 2 + 3 = 7 - 2 - 3$. As the first two terms on each side of the equal sign are exactly the same, we can remove them, hence we have: $3 = -3$.

We know $3 = -3$ is false. Because we are certain that $7 - 2 - 3 = 2$ is true, we can conclude that $7 - 2 + 3 = 2$ is the part that leads to this contradiction and, therefore, it's false.

By our second method, let's use a real-world scenario. Suppose you had \$7 in your bank account. On a particular day, you left home for the bank and deposited \$3 there, and stopped by a convenience store and made a purchase of \$2 using this bank account, and then headed home. Once home, you calculated your new account balance: $7 + 3 - 2 = 8$, meaning you had \$8 on your account. No doubt about it.

Let's backtrack a little and suppose you wanted to do all this over but in a different sequence. Again, you had a beginning balance of \$7, and you wanted to deposit \$3 and spend \$2, but you wanted to stop at the convenience

Figure 7.1 A Modified Model for the Order of Operations. M and D are on the same level and neither has precedence over the other. So are A and S.

$$\begin{array}{c} \text{P} \\ \text{E} \\ \text{M D} \\ \text{A S} \end{array}$$

store first to make the $2 purchase and then deposit $3 at the bank. After your trip, again, you wanted to calculate your account balance. So, $7 - 2 + 3 = ?$

If someone told you that your ending balance was $2 (because that person claimed that $7 - 2 + 3 = 2$), you wouldn't believe it. "What? Just because I made the purchase first my ending balance isn't $8?" Or you would argue in another perspective, "Listen, I had $7 before the trip. I deposited more than I spent. How come I ended up having even less money than I started with?"

You get the picture.

"If PEMDAS is misleading, how should I go about teaching the order of operations?" you may ask. A simple modification of the presentation of the six operations (or symbols) will do the job. Instead of presenting them in a linear, sequential manner, rearrange them into four levels, as shown in Figure 7.1.

There are two rules regarding the interpretation of the order of operations exemplified in this model:

1. Higher-level operations take precedence over lower-level ones, and
2. if two or more operations are on the same level, they must be carried out from left to right.

(Of course when all operations are addition or all operations are multiplication, we have the freedom of doing whichever operation first. In such cases the result will be the same, per the associative property.)

The three Math in Action boxes that follow present sample problems solved according to these rules, with explanations provided after each step.

 Math in Action: Sample Problem 1

$12 + 6 \div 2$
$= 12 + 3$ (Division is on a higher level than addition. Division first.)
$= 15$

Math in Action: Sample Problem 2

$6 \div 2 \times 9$

$= 3 \times 9$ (Multiplication and division are on the same level. From left to right.)

$= 27$

 Math in Action: Sample Problem 3

$-24 \div (4 - 7) - 12 + 5 \, (-2)^3$

$= -24 \div (-3) - 12 + 5 \, (-2)^3$ (Parenthesis comes first.*)

$= -24 \div (-3) - 12 + 5 \, (-8)$ (Exponent comes next.)

$= 8 - 12 + 5 \, (-8)$ (Division higher than addition/subtraction, and is on the same level with multiplication. Division first.)

$= 8 - 12 + (-40)$ (Multiplication higher than addition/subtraction.† Multiplication first.)

$= -4 + (-40)$ (Addition and subtraction are on the same level. From left to right.)

$= -44$

* Actually, since $(4 - 7)$ and $(-2)^3$ don't cross over to each other, either of them can be executed first, or both can be executed within the same step, without affecting the final result.

† The multiplication sign is omitted between 5 and the following term.

The key point is, stop teaching "Please Excuse My Dear Aunt Sally" immediately. Never say the order of operations is PEMDAS. It's utterly misleading and untrue. If it helps you to remember, just think Aunt Sally is evil and you should never excuse her.

The Order "M/D before A/S" Isn't Haphazard

After Jane started teaching the order of operations, she quickly discovered that it's a great hurdle for her children to overcome because they, out of the habit they have formed so far of processing written information from left to right, tend to solve a mathematical problem from left to right, so that their answer is 20 for $2 + 3 \times 4$. For them to do 3×4 first before doing the addition part squarely contradicts their habit: When they read, they read from left to right. When they write, they write from left to right. And now many of them feel puzzled when they suddenly have to start solving certain problems from the middle!

So Jane found herself saying this to her children one day: "We have to use some order to carry out mathematical operations when there are two or more of them in a problem, otherwise different people may come up with different answers. Nobody knows why, but mathematicians have decided that multiplication and division should be executed before addition and subtraction."

Believe it or not, the order that multiplication and division come before addition and subtraction was not decided on haphazardly. There is a reason for this order. Let's use a real-world situation to explain this.

Suppose you are shopping in a grocery store and have put some items in your cart, as shown in the following Math in Action box.

☑ Math in Action: A List of Groceries for Purchase

Item	Unit Price	Quantity
Bread	$2.50	3 bags
Milk	$2.89	2 bottles
Cookies	$3.99	5 boxes
Water	$0.99	6 bottles
Juice	$1.75	6 bottles
Cereal	$3.50	4 boxes
Orange	$0.65	8 pieces

To make sure that you have enough money on you to pay for these items, you want to know the total amount of money for these items. You take out your TI-30 calculator and punch in the following:

$$2.50 \times 3 + 2.89 \times 2 + 3.99 \times 5 + 0.99 \times 6 + 1.75 \times 6 + 3.50 \times 4 + 0.65 \times 8$$

You then hit the = key and the total is displayed instantly as 68.87. In other words, the calculator first computes 2.50 × 3, puts the result somewhere in its memory, then computes the next type of items, 2.89 × 2, and again puts the result somewhere in its memory. The same procedure is repeated for all remaining items, and then it sums up the amounts for all individual types of items and displays the total.

Let's suppose the operations did not have this order. Instead, all operations should be carried out from left to right. For the example problem, the calculator (or a human being, for this matter) would first do the leftmost operation, 2.50×3, and get 7.50. This is the amount of money for bread, and it's fine so far. The calculator would proceed to the next operation, $7.50 + 2.89$ and get 10.39. Well, this doesn't make much sense. What is the meaning of adding the unit price of milk to the amount of money needed for 3 bags of bread? The next step would be even more irrational: 10.39×2. What does the result mean? Before long, the calculations would get out of hand, and a correct amount of money for the groceries would never be reached. Simply put, carrying out operations simply from left to right wouldn't work in many cases. There definitely should be a certain order by the type of operation.

Let's look at a different scenario. Suppose the order of operations was addition before multiplication (to make things simpler, let's leave out subtraction and division). After all, children learn addition first and then multiplication—and you might wonder, wouldn't it make more sense to carry out addition before multiplication? Again, let's refer to the grocery list problem and see how that would turn out. If, as before, you punched in the numbers this way:

$$2.50 \times 3 + 2.89 \times 2 + 3.99 \times 5 + 0.99 \times 6 + 1.75 \times 6 + 3.50 \times 4 + 0.65 \times 8$$

the calculator wouldn't be able to produce the correct amount of money. In an "addition before multiplication" order, the calculator would first do $3 + 2.89$. But that doesn't make sense: What does the quantity of bread plus the unit price of milk mean? In other words, what do you call the result—5.89 bags, or 5.89 dollars? Again, it wouldn't give us the amount we want.

To obtain the correct amount of money with either "order," that is, the "from left to right" order or the "addition before multiplication" order, we would have to use parentheses. Therefore, we would need to key in this sequence on a calculator:

$$(2.50 \times 3) + (2.89 \times 2) + (3.99 \times 5) + (0.99 \times 6) + (1.75 \times 6) + (3.50 \times 4)$$
$$+ (0.65 \times 8)$$

This would work. But think about how much trouble it would be to have to enter a pair of parentheses for each type of groceries you had picked. The example list contained only 7 items. If your grocery list was 200 types of items long (not unheard of), you would have to literally enter 200 pairs of parentheses. It would be very time consuming and prone to error to do this.

Thus, it all boils down to this: With the order of operations we have, for situations like the grocery list problem, there is no need to use parentheses—this order is simpler, saves time, and less error prone.

You may ask, "Aren't there situations where people have to add before they multiply? In such situations, wouldn't it make as much sense to stipulate an 'addition before multiplication' order as a 'multiplication before addition' order?"

Certainly there are such situations, such as this scenario: "Ms. Smith teaches 3 second-grade classes, and there are 18, 25, and 22 children in these classes. If she needs to collect $5 from each child for the upcoming field trip, what is the total amount of money she has to collect?" If the order of operations were "addition before multiplication", then either $18 + 25 + 22 \times 5$ or $5 \times 18 + 25 + 22$ would take care of it, and we wouldn't have to use parentheses.

However, such situations are far less common than those such as calculating the total sum of money for a list of groceries. In fact, unlike the grocery list scenario—where you can create a list as long as you want it to be (the general manager of a grocery store could literally sum up the value of all the inventory of that store—thousands of types of commodities, on a handheld calculator, if he or she so chooses and if the calculator has enough memory, without using a single pair of parentheses)—it's very difficult, if not impossible, to imagine a long list where all additions would need to be computed *before* all the resulting sums multiplied. Try coming up with a story problem to fit $23 + 50 \times 31 + 29 \times 27 + 99 \times 54 + 75$, where addition needs to be executed before multiplication, and you'll realize there aren't many such situations. Adopting an "addition before multiplication" order would make it necessary to use parentheses in all those omnipresent grocery list-type situations, and that would be very counterproductive.

This is precisely the underlying reason why multiplication should come before addition: It is simpler and saves time. Mathematicians didn't simply pick multiplication over addition in specifying the order of operations. There was a reason to do so.

Next time you go shopping, try using a pair of parentheses for every type of items in calculating the total amount of money needed. Then you will start to appreciate the rule mathematicians have set up for us: multiplication comes before addition.

Are *Negative* and *Subtract* Really Different?

Just recently, Jane learned that the correct order of operations stipulates that addition and subtraction are on the same level and should be performed from left to right, and so are multiplication and division. This was fine now, but then she encountered a new problem: The order of operations doesn't say anything about the negative sign. So, based on her understanding, this is what Jane told her children one day about how to solve $-3^2 + 5$: "We have exponent and addition in this problem. What do we do first?" After she got confirmation from her children, Jane finished the problem in this way: $-3^2 + 5 = 9 + 5 = 14$. In other words, she squared -3 first, and got 9. Then adding 5 to it, she got 14.

Unfortunately, this is incorrect. The first part of the problem, -3^2, actually has two operations involved: a subtraction and an exponent. We know exponents come before subtraction, and for that part, the result is: $-3^2 = -9$.

You might protest, "That's a negative sign! It's not a subtraction sign!"

But aren't they the same thing?

They are.

Treating the negative sign and the subtraction sign as different may be the underlying reason that many people miscalculate the problem just described. Since there is no mention of the negative sign in the rule governing the order of operations, many people assume this negative sign isn't part of the picture. So Jane, not surprisingly, considered this negative sign and 3 as if they were "fused" together, and that's why her result was a positive 9.

In reality, no matter how you write the negative sign (that is, right at the middle position or a little higher above the middle position) and no matter how you say it (be it *negative*, *minus*, or *subtract*), it is the same thing. What applies to "subtract" applies to "negative." That's why for the problem described, the negative sign has to wait until the exponent is executed. If, however, you want to square the whole quantity of -3, you have to put it in parentheses, as in $(-3)^2 = 9$. This is very similar to the relationship between multiplication and addition, where multiplication takes precedence over addition, as in $2 + 3 \times 4 = 2 + 12 = 14$. If, however, you want addition to be performed first, you have to resort to parentheses, as in $(2 + 3) \times 4 = 5 \times 4 = 20$.

If you have a stubborn habit of wanting to square the whole quantity of -3 when you see -3^2, here's something you can do. When you are presented with -3^2, first put a different number before it. Then you solve the problem as you would normally do. After you're done, then remove whatever you have put there. Let's suppose you see -3^2 and you aren't so sure about whether to square the whole quantity or the 3 only. You put a number, say 5^2, before it, and now it has become $5^2 - 3^2$. You won't have any problem performing the next step for this problem: $5^2 - 3^2 = 25 - 9$ (you don't want to say the sign before 9 has now become positive, do you?). Since you have put a number there as a helper, you need to remove it now. So remove 5^2, which has become 25, and you should have -9 left as the result of -3^2.

So from now on, first convince yourself that $-3^2 = -9$, and then convince yourself that *negative*, *minus*, and *subtract* are all the same mathematically.

8

Algebra

An Equal Sign Means Equal

It's very often the case that there's more than one operation in an arithmetic expression, and solving it naturally requires several steps. Here's what Jane showed her children about how to evaluate $9 \times 4 + 7 - 5 + 1$, as shown in the following Math in Action box.

> ☑ **Math in Action: A Problem Jane Solved**
>
> $9 \times 4 + 7 - 5 + 1$
> $= 36 + 7$
> $= 43 - 5$
> $= 38 + 1$
> $= 39$

While the final answer was correct, there was a serious problem with the process. Specifically, Jane used equal signs to connect expressions that are not equal. She simply wrote the result of the first operation and then brought down the next operation, disregarding what the whole problem says or what each intermediate step equals to. To have a better idea of where her mistake lies, let's first evaluate what each of the three middle lines equals to and see if it justifies the use of an equal sign (see the following Math in Action box).

> ☑ **Math in Action: The Three Middle Lines Are Problematic**
>
> Line 1: $9 \times 4 + 7 - 5 + 1$
> Line 2: $36 + 7 \, (= 43)$
> Line 3: $43 - 5 \, (= 38)$
> Line 4: $38 + 1 \, (= 39)$
> Line 5: 39

All the three intermediate steps lead to different results. Therefore, it's a mistake to connect them with an equal sign. It's as preposterous as saying "one equals two."

Jane may feel tempted to claim that she got the correct answer anyway. To discredit this claim, we need to take a look at what effect this illogicality of using equal signs has on children's future learning of mathematics, for there's a long journey lying ahead of them handling more sophisticated math problems than just finding the correct answer for a simple expression as $9 \times 4 + 7 - 5 + 1$. Two broad math topics can be negatively affected by this mistake. The first one is children's future learning of solving equations. We know that in the process of solving an equation, one of the key notions is to isolate a variable by adding, subtracting, multiplying, or dividing by a certain quantity as long as we do it to *both* sides of the equation. This is very much like balancing scales. If we put a weight on one side without putting a comparable weight on the other side of the scale, it will become unbalanced. Connecting expressions that are not equal directly runs afoul of this key notion, causing the two sides of an equation to be "unbalanced."

The second topic to be affected is doing mathematical proofs. Take one method of proof, proof by contradiction, for example. Here let's refer back to an actual proof we did at the beginning of Chapter 7 when we were discussing the order of operations. We first assumed that $7 - 2 + 3 = 2$ is true. Then after introducing into the proving process the indisputably true statement $7 - 2 - 3 = 2$, we found that if both statements were true, then it must follow that $3 = -3$. Because of this contradiction, we concluded that $7 - 2 + 3 = 2$ is false. In this process, all that matters is the truth value of a statement: for example, $1 + 2 = 3$ is true but $3 = -3$ is false. If children have difficulty telling false statements from true ones, they will certainly have difficulty doing mathematical proofs.

In addition, Jane's way of evaluating the first operation before bringing down the second operation will not work properly if all the operations are not in a left-to-right manner, as in:

$$18 - 5 \times 3 + 12 \div 6$$
$$= 15 \ldots$$

Even though the first number, 18, should be skipped for the moment, after the execution of 5×3, Jane really could not go any further from there, because the next operation is not immediately after 15. This is where errors can easily occur.

Here's a lesson to draw: Use equal signs only between expressions that are equal. In this regard, this is the rule applicable to all expressions, whether they should be carried out from left to right or whether they are in a not-so-organized order. What's more important, this will lay a solid foundation for children's future learning of other math topics such as solving equations and doing proofs.

With that said, the proper way of evaluating the two problems discussed earlier is shown in the Math in Action boxes that follow.

> ☑ **Math in Action: The Proper Way of Evaluating Jane's Sample Problem**
>
> $9 \times 4 + 7 - 5 + 1$
> $= 36 + 7 - 5 + 1$
> $= 43 - 5 + 1$
> $= 38 + 1$
> $= 39$

> ☑ **Math in Action: The Proper Way of Evaluating a Problem not Quite "Organized"**
>
> $18 - 5 \times 3 + 12 \div 6$
> $= 18 - 15 + 12 \div 6$
> $= 18 - 15 + 2$
> $= 3 + 2$
> $= 5$

What Does Adding Up Numbers Landed Have to Do with Finding Factors?

After teaching factors, Jane gave her children an exercise to do. First she gave each child a worksheet with numbers 1–100 listed sequentially, each in a square, with 1 at the "Start" point and 100 at the "Finish" point. Then she divided her children into groups of two and instructed them to roll a dice, go to a number, underline it with a colored marker, and then write out all factors this underlined number has. The two children in each group should take turns (using different-colored markers) until one of them reached the end of the list. At this point, they would need to add up all the underlined numbers, and the child with the larger sum would be considered the winner.

The following Math in Action box shows the work of Tom and Megan. For the sake of brevity, only numbers 44 through 53 are shown.

☑️ **Math in Action: Megan Won This Game for Landing Numbers That Have a Larger Sum**

Tom

44: 1, 2, 4, 11, 22, 44
45: 1, 3, 5, 9, 15, 45
46:
47
48: 1, 2, 3, 4, 6, 8, 12, 16, 24, 48
49
50
51
52
53

Sum of underlined numbers:

44 + 45 + 48 = 137

Megan

44
45
46
47: 1, 17
48

49
50
51: 1, 3, 17, 51
52
53: 1, 53

Sum of underlined numbers:

47 + 51 + 53 = 151

For the selected part of the game, Megan won, as the sum of the three numbers landed was 151, larger than Tom's sum, 137.

Seems to be an interesting game, doesn't it? But here is a problem: What does adding up all the underlined numbers have to do with finding factors? The instructional focus of this lesson apparently was finding factors, but adding up all numbers landed drifted away from this focus into something children had dealt with much earlier: finding the sum of 2-digit numbers. In other words, when they added up the underlined numbers, they didn't even have to look at what factors they had found. A winning-conscious child (and most of them are at this age) would soon discover that what factors a number contains really didn't matter in winning the game. A better chance was simply to land on larger numbers.

Thus, the focus of this game should be changed back to factors. Instead of telling her children to find the sum of all the numbers landed, what Jane needed to do was tell them to find the number of factors for each number landed, write down that number to the right of those factors, and then find the grand total of all the factors found. The child with the higher total number of factors wins. The following Math in Action box shows how the worksheet of the game would look based on the revised game plan.

☑ **Math in Action: Tom Won This Game for Having Landed on Numbers Containing More Factors**

Tom
44: 1, 2, 4, 11, 22, 44 (6 factors)
45: 1, 3, 5, 9, 15, 45 (6 factors)
46
47
48: 1, 2, 3, 4, 6, 8, 12, 16, 24, 48 (10 factors)

49
50
51
52
53

Total number of factors:

6 + 6 + 10 = 22

Megan
44
45
46
<u>47</u>: 1, 47 (2 factors)
48
49
50
<u>51</u>: 1, 3, 17, 51 (4 factors)
52
<u>53</u>: 1, 53 (2 factors)

Total number of factors:

2 + 4 + 2 = 8

By this revised game plan, Tom won the game for landing on numbers that had a total of 22 factors. Megan had landed on numbers that generated only 8 factors. In order to win this game, a child has to land on numbers with more factors than those with fewer factors. Now, with this revised game plan, Jane's children would need to know what numbers are "factor-rich" and what numbers are "factor-poor."

This small change will result in a positive effect in helping children handle the concept they are learning at this time: two numbers of a similar magnitude may contain very different numbers of factors: For example, 47 has only 2 factors while 48 has 10.

The benefits actually don't just stop here. A good understanding of a number and its factors can help children build a solid foundation for learning at least the following two topics:

1. Simplifying fractions. If the denominator and numerator have a common factor (except for the number 1), then this fraction can be

simplified by this factor. To use the worksheet Jane had used as an example, both 45 and 48 have 3 as their common factor. If a fraction has these two numbers in it such as $\frac{45}{48}$, then this fraction can be simplified by this common factor. Furthermore, if the two numbers in a fraction have two or more common factors, then using a larger common factor will involve fewer steps and thus saves time. For example, 44 and 48 have two common factors: 2 and 4. Simplifying a fraction having these two numbers such as $\frac{44}{48}$ by 4 involves fewer steps.

2. Distinguishing between prime and composite numbers. It'll be very easy to extend from a "factor-poor" number to a prime number, defined as a number having 1 and itself as its only factors. In the worksheet Jane had used, 47 and 53 have only 2 factors each, and thus they are prime numbers. In contrast, those "factor-rich" numbers can be easily redefined as composite numbers, those having three or more factors, such as 44, 45, and 48.

Timelines Aren't Good Candidates for Teaching Negative Numbers

To introduce her children to the concept of negative numbers, Jane decided to relate it to their daily life as closely as possible. She already has a school calendar on the wall, and the first thing she does each morning is to have her children indicate the number of days that school has been in session ("Today is day 1" for the first day of school, "Today is day 2" for the second day of school, and so on). So she decided to capitalize on this calendar. She said to her children, "Imagine school starts tomorrow and you're preparing for it. Tomorrow would be day 1 because that's the first day of school. Then today is one day before school starts, we'll call it day −1. Yesterday was two days before school starts, so it is −2 . . . ."

A problem with using a timeline to model negative numbers is that it doesn't exactly signify the concept of a number line: A key element, 0, is missing. In other words, if school starts tomorrow and today is represented as day −1, then you would have to jump from day −1 to day 1, with no day 0 between today and tomorrow.

Because of this missing 0, calculations involving timelines can be erroneous. Let's use some examples to explain this.

People usually use subtraction to figure out the length of time that has elapsed between two points of time. For example, in figuring out the number of years between 1989 and 2016, subtraction will do the job nicely: 2016 − 1989 = 27.

In fact, this is the most common way to calculate a person's age. When these dates don't span 0, there's no problem at all. However, because of the missing 0 that separate the dates before and the dates after, calculations of two dates that span 0 won't work. Using the same school calendar example, there are 2 days between day 1 and day 3 (3 − 1 = 2). This is correct. But if we shift the starting date one day ahead of time and ask how many days there are between day −1 and day 3, we know there are 3 days. But if we use the formula as we would regularly use, we would reach a wrong result: 3 − (−1) = 4.

The same problem would appear in other measurements of time when it goes back beyond the reference point of the calendar era currently in use. Case in point: There's no year between year 1 BCE and year 1 CE in this year-numbering system. That means an event would be either on the CE side or the BCE side, with no neutral year, namely, year 0, in between. Technically, subtraction between two dates that span this "turn" will yield a result that is off by 1. But people seldom notice this problem because calculation involving this reference point, dating back more than 2000 years, is hardly needed in daily life. Sometimes when we do need to refer to events dating back that early in time such as referring to artifacts crafted around that time or earlier, approximate numbers are usually sufficient. Under this circumstance, a difference of 1 is really insignificant and negligible. For example, if archeologists unearthed, in year 2000 CE, an item that was supposedly crafted in year 1000 BCE, how old was it in year 2000 CE? We say it was 3000 years old, as 2000 − (−1000) = 3000. However, this isn't totally correct. If those two dates were exact, then the actual age was 2999 years. This is because 999 years elapsed between year 1000 BCE and year 1 BCE, and 1999 years elapsed between year 1 CE and year 2000 CE, but only 1 year elapsed between year 1 BCE and year 1 CE. Adding up those three lengths of time, we have: 999 + 1 + 1999 = 2999. This can be illustrated with Figure 8.1.

Such an incongruity often goes undetected, as mentioned earlier, because of the small difference in contrast with the large, approximate time span. However, if we focus on a short time period that spans only this turn of millenniums, the mistake could be jarring. For example, if a political movement started in summer, year 1 BCE and lasted till summer, year 1 CE, and if

Figure 8.1 The Length of Time Between 1000 BCE and 2000 CE Is 2999 Years

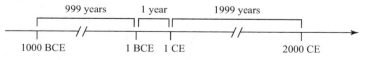

Note: figure not drawn to scale

someone stated the movement lasted for two years because $1 - (-1) = 2$, that would make a huge historical error.

Because timelines with this missing 0 don't fare well in calculating an exact answer between two points of time around it, they aren't good candidates for use in teaching elementary children about negative numbers. Although at the beginning stage it would seem fine when you want to refer to "one day before school starts" as day −1, and "two days before school starts" as day −2, the real problem will surface as soon as you start to calculate the length of time that has elapsed. Since this is something that children will soon spend time on, it'll be necessary to find things that have a 0 between positive and negative values. In this regard, a thermometer or a person's bank account are ideal candidates. In other words, there is a $0°$ in temperature and there is a balance of 0 in one's bank account. A room with a temperature of $1°$ is $2°$ warmer than another room with a temperature of $−1°$, and compared with a person with a balance of −$1, if Jane has a balance of $1, then she is $2 richer. Between these two candidates, a thermometer is particularly good in that it's visually analogous to a number line: Lay down a thermometer in centigrade reading (it usually contains $0°$) horizontally with the higher numbers on the right side and you have a bona fide number line.

The Worst Example in Teaching Exponents

It was time for her children to learn exponents. Jane explained the meaning of the "small 2" raised to the upper right corner of the base number, telling them that it was an exponent. She then presented with this example: $2^2 = 4$.

This is the worst example in teaching exponents. Let's see why.

An exponent means the number of times a quantity is to be multiplied. For example, if we want to multiply four 5s, namely, $5 \times 5 \times 5 \times 5$, we can express this as 5^4. Here 5 is called the *base* and 4 is called the *exponent*. At the beginning stage many teachers would have their children practice on writing out the expanded form of 5^4 before writing the result, as: $5^4 = 5 \times 5 \times 5 \times 5 = 625$. This is because children at this time have a tendency to interpret 5^4 as 5×4. This tendency will linger for a while before they will gradually grasp the meaning of exponents. This intermediate step of writing the expanded form is meant to help children understand the meaning of exponents and not to form the misconception of interpreting 5^4 as 5×4. However, the use of $2^2 = 4$ as a beginning example is instilling in children exactly the misconception they should avoid forming.

Let's trace the mind work of children who have just been exposed to exponents. At this beginning stage, some children may use the "face value" of what they see and interpret the 4 in 5^4 as a factor (5×4) instead of as the number of factors (four such factors, namely, $5 \times 5 \times 5 \times 5$, where there is not a 4 visible on the surface). When they see that the result of $5^4 = 625$ contradicts their face-value interpretation ($5 \times 4 = 20$), they are forced to abandon the face-value interpretation and reconsider the definition of an exponent. Gradually they will adopt the correct interpretation of exponents and are on their way to handling expressions containing exponents.

But the example of $2^2 = 4$ perfectly matches their incorrect, face-value interpretation. Even though they may have been told many times what the "small 2" means, they see two 2s, take the base for the first factor and the exponent for the second factor, multiply them, and get the right answer ($2 \times 2 = 4$)! This will simply reinforce their incorrect interpretation, and they will probably continue to produce answers like $3^2 = 6$, $4^2 = 8$, and so on. In other words, they are not starting off on a solid ground. Later they will have to spend time unlearning this misconception.

You may ask, what's a good example to use in teaching exponents? The answer is, any other number will work as long as its magnitude is low so that children can see the meaning of exponent easily, such as $3^2 = 9$ ($3 \times 2 \neq 9$), $4^2 = 16$ ($4 \times 2 \neq 16$), and $5^3 = 125$ ($5 \times 3 \neq 125$).

9

Geometry: Bits and Pieces

Don't Count the Diagonals on a Grid

When Jane was teaching *perimeter*, she drew a few geometric figures on a grid. Then she told her children what perimeter was and that in order to find it, they needed to count the spaces on the grid for each side and then add up all these sides. Her first figure was a rectangle (see Figure 9.1). Her children counted the four sides to be 4, 6, 4, and 6 units. Next, she had them add up these lengths and they got $4 + 6 + 4 + 6 = 20$ units.

The next figure was a triangle. Jane and her children counted all three sides to be 5, 5, and 5 units and thus they calculated the perimeter to be $5 + 5 + 5 = 15$ units (see Figure 9.2).

This is a mistake. After all, if all the three sides of a triangle were 5 units each, it would have been an equilateral triangle, and the triangle Jane drew was apparently not. It could be reasoned that all the three angles in an equilateral triangle are $60°$ each, and the triangle Jane drew had a right angle, with two of its sides coinciding with the grid lines. If a triangle isn't equilateral, then all the three sides are not congruent. So we can conclude that for the triangle shown in Figure 9.2, it's certainly *not* the case that all the three sides are 5 units each.

You may ask, "I can see that the two legs of this triangle are 5 units each. But how long is its hypotenuse if it's not 5?" To answer this question, let's take one square from the grid and see (see Figure 9.3).

Figure 9.1 For This Rectangle, the Perimeter Is 4 + 6 + 4 + 6 = 20 Units

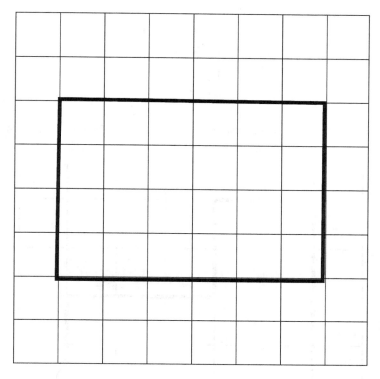

Figure 9.2 For This Triangle, the Perimeter Is Not 15 Units. Specifically, the hypotenuse is not 5 units.

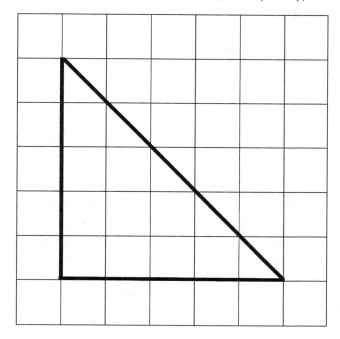

Figure 9.3 For an Isosceles Right Triangle as This One, the Hypotenuse Is √2 Units Long

Figure 9.4 For Lower Grades, a Simpler Way Is to Use Horizontal and Vertical Line Segments Only

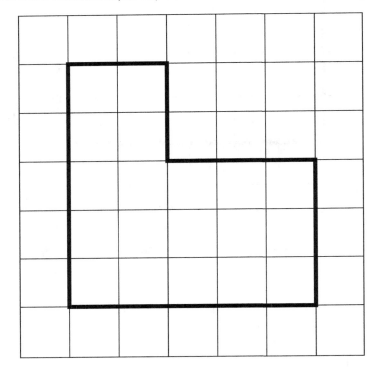

In this triangle, the two legs are 1 unit each. By Pythagorean theorem, for any right triangle, $a^2 + b^2 = c^2$, and therefore $c = \sqrt{a^2 + b^2}$, with a and b being the two legs and c being the hypotenuse of such a triangle. Thus, $c = \sqrt{a^2 + b^2} = \sqrt{1^2 + 1^2} = \sqrt{1+1} = \sqrt{2}$ (you can find on a calculator that $\sqrt{2}$ is about 1.4). This is the ratio for any isosceles right triangle (cutting a square along one of the diagonals will give you two such triangles). In other words, if the two legs of a right triangle are congruent, then the ratio of the three sides of this triangle (leg : leg : hypotenuse) is $1 : 1 : \sqrt{2}$.

As the hypotenuse in Jane's original triangle is 5 times this length, it's $5 \times \sqrt{2} \approx 5 \times 1.4 \approx 7$, about 2 units longer than Jane thought it to be.

Now that we know that all the three sides of a right triangle, as drawn on a grid, are not congruent, how should we go about teaching children how to find the perimeter of a triangle? One way is to cut a grid into strips and have each child use a strip as a ruler to measure the distance. This, however, may be a challenging task if your children are in primary grades and not experienced in measuring yet. Another issue your children will encounter is having to round, as the hypotenuse of most triangles drawn on a grid will be unlikely to end up being whole units.

For lower-grade children, a simpler way would be to draw figures on the grid's horizontal and vertical line segments only (see Figure 9.4). After all, the focus of this lesson is perimeter, and you want to get this concept across without your children having to deal with measuring at the same time.

"All 3-D Shapes Have an Extra Third Dimension of Height"

After her children had enough experience with 2-D shapes, Jane started exposing them to 3-D ones. Naturally, she based her discussion of 3-D shapes on their knowledge of 2-D shapes. She said, "A rectangle is a two-dimensional shape, and it has two dimensions of length and width. A rectangular prism is a three-dimensional shape, and it has three dimensions of length, width, and height. So we can say all three-dimensional shapes have an extra third dimension of height."

But Jane didn't have a ready answer when a child asked, "When I look at a triangle, it's a two-dimensional shape and its two dimensions are base and height. Now if I have a triangular prism, it's a three-dimensional shape. Then what's its third dimension? Is it another height? If so, how is it different from the previous height? Or should we think base is no longer a dimension, and now we must say that a triangle has length and width, but not base and height?"

The child's questions are legitimate. It's Jane's definition of all 3-D shapes having a third dimension of *height* that's problematic. Apparently Jane rank ordered *length*, *width*, and *height* and saved the last word, *height*, for her "third" dimension. But she ran into trouble when she had a 2-D triangle that already has a "height."

First of all, "two-dimensional" and "three-dimensional" are just different aspects of things we perceive or describe. This isn't like the case where people first invented the clock to tell time and later added a special feature of "alarm" for waking someone up. It's difficult to imagine the initial invention of an alarm clock without a regular clock having been there already. In this sense, we may say that an alarm clock is a regular clock with an additional feature of alarms. In contrast, 2-D shapes and 3-D shapes have always been there. It just depends on the perspective in which we want to describe them (although of course children learn 2-D shapes before they learn 3-D ones). For example, if you plan to hang a string across your room for hanging decorations on, you'll need to know the distance across your room. This is 1-D. Suppose you want to lay carpet for that same room: You'll need to find out its area. This is 2-D. Further suppose you want to use that same room for storing as many same-size boxes as you can: You will have to find out its space, or volume. This is 3-D. Your room is the same room. Depending on whether you want to hang a string, lay a carpet, or store boxes, you are looking at it as one-dimensional, two-dimensional, or three-dimensional.

Now let's consider two scenarios to give *height* a close look. For the first one, suppose you're looking at the floor of your room and thinking about its area in terms of *length* and *width*. Then after a while you are looking at your room as storage space and you add a third dimension, *height*. For the second scenario, let's suppose you're thinking about buying a tapestry and now you're looking at one of the walls in your room in terms of *length* and *height*. When you want to consider the whole space and switch to the third dimension, you will find that *height* has been used and there is only *width* left. If, however, you're thinking about the wall as being *length* by *width*, then your *height* will be horizontal. But the real issue is, does it matter for what you call the "third" dimension? Or does it matter if your height is not upright but rather from side to side? Certainly, it doesn't. In this sense, there's no order in which one of the three terms, namely, *length, width,* and *height,* should be used only after the other two have been used. Let's say you have a book in front of you with the dimensions 20 cm × 30 cm × 5 cm. You can name whichever side length, whichever side width, and whichever side height. If you want to describe the front cover, you can say "length" and "width." But it's just as legitimate if you call them "width" and "height." Can you call the 5-centimeter side the "length"? Of course you can if you want, and there's nothing that says you can't.

The simplest way to avoid getting yourself into the dilemma described earlier is to avoid specifying *height* being the third dimension. It can be *height*, but it can also be *length* or *width*, depending on which you prefer. For the triangular prism problem that one of Jane's children asked about, since *base* and *height* have been used, she may use *length* to refer to the third dimension (as if the triangular prism is laid down sideways)—or she may use *width* just as well.

In short, you may want to get out of the mindset of "order" in which height must be used for the third dimension. Then it will be much easier to explain the difference between 2-D and 3-D shapes to your children.

Don't Use "Vertical" to Find the Horizontal Value

During a lesson on coordinate geometry, Jane described to her children how to plot a point on the coordinate system. She said, "A point is represented by an ordered pair such as (5, 2). Here the first number represents the *x*-value and the second number represents the *y*-value. To plot such a point, first look at the *x*-value and count that many vertical points on the horizontal line. Then look at the *y*-value and count that many horizontal points on the vertical line" (see Figure 9.5).

While this might work for her, the way she said it can be confusing to her children. In locating and plotting a point on the coordinate system, direction is of utmost importance. The position of the coordinates indicated in an ordered pair dictates which direction to go. The *x*-value is always written first, before the comma, and is to be located horizontally on the coordinate system. The *y*-value always comes second, after the comma, and is to be located vertically on the coordinate system. Mixing up these two directions can easily cause children to make mistakes, as (5, 2) and (2, 5) are different points. When Jane said to find the *x*-coordinate (5, in this example)

Figure 9.5 An Ordered Pair (5, 2) Plotted on the Coordinate System

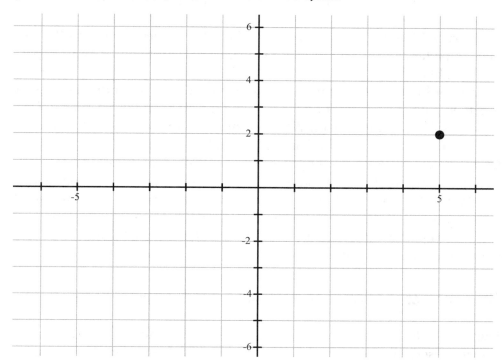

Figure 9.6 A Number Line With 5 Plotted

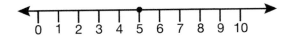

her children needed to "count 5 vertical points on the horizontal line" she mentioned both "vertical" and "horizontal." Then when she said to find the *y*-coordinate (2) they needed to "count two horizontal points on the vertical line," again she mentioned both "vertical" and "horizontal." When it's time for her children to plot some points on their own, some of them may wonder, "Which is which?"

To give children a solid grasp of the position indicated by the two numbers in an ordered pair and help them avoid mixing the two coordinates, we need to tie the word *horizontal* to the *x*-axis only, without saying the word *vertical*. Similarly, we need to tie the word *vertical* to the *y*-axis only without mentioning the word *horizontal*.

You might ask, "Won't I be handicapped without using *vertical* when I need to talk about locating the point on the *x*-axis?" Not at all. As a matter of fact, Jane's saying "Count 5 vertical points on the horizontal line" when plotting (5, 2) was based on a misconception. She was misled by those vertical lines. To make this clearer, let's plot 5 on a regular number line (see Figure 9.6).

Here you probably wouldn't say, "Count 5 vertical points to the right of 0." A better choice of word to use here is *spaces* or *units*, as "Count 5 spaces to the right of 0."

A coordinate system is nothing more than two regular number lines put together, with one laid out horizontally and the other laid out vertically, intersecting at 0 for both of them. When plotting the first number of an ordered pair, we need to focus on the horizontal number line only, without being distracted by the vertical lines that pass through this line, and simply say, "Count 5 *spaces* to the right of 0 (if that number is positive) on the horizontal line." Similarly, when plotting the second number of this ordered pair, we need to focus on the vertical number line without being distracted by the horizontal lines passing through it and say, "Count 2 *spaces* up from 0 (again, if that number is positive) on the vertical line."

The Two Sides of a Symmetrical Figure Aren't Exactly the Same

During her lesson on line symmetry—the most common form of symmetry discussed in elementary school classrooms—Jane gave this definition:

Figure 9.7 A Figure Isn't Necessarily Symmetrical When Its Two Sides Are the Same

"Symmetry means *the same*. When a figure is symmetrical, it means its two sides are exactly the same along the line in the middle."

This definition is problematic. To see why, let's use a simple figure to illustrate (see Figure 9.7).

In this figure, there is a bird on either side of the line in the middle, and the two birds are exactly the same with respect to their shape, size, and layout. But is this figure symmetrical along the line in the middle? By the definition Jane gave, her children would be led into thinking that it is because the two birds fit her definition of being "the same." In reality, however, this figure is not symmetrical.

To properly define line symmetry, you have to stress what constitutes the most essential feature. Depending on the age of your children, you may do one of several things. For younger children, you may demonstrate cutting out a symmetrical figure on a piece of paper. First fold the paper to make a crease. Then draw a figure along the crease, preferably a half figure such as half of a butterfly or half of a tree. Cut out the figure and then unfold the paper. What your children see is a symmetrical figure along the crease. The point here is to demonstrate to your children that when the figure is folded along the crease, one side of the cutout matches the other.

If your children are old enough to know the meaning of *mirror image*, that will be a great phrase to use to explain the meaning of line symmetry. To aid your children in the understanding of this concept, you may demonstrate by putting a mirror beside a simple figure, a paper cutout, and so on, and let your children see the actual figure or cutout and its reflection in the mirror. These two corresponding parts form a symmetrical figure. For example, if you have a bird cutout and then have a mirror image beside it along the edge of the mirror, they will form a symmetrical figure. Then you may transfer this demonstration onto the board by drawing two birds facing each other along a line in the middle, as in Figure 9.8.

Now your children can see that the two parts of a symmetrical figure are not simply "the same," but that they need to be a mirror image of each other. Because a mirror image is a reflection, line symmetry is also called reflection symmetry.

Figure 9.8 A Figure Is Symmetrical When Its Two Sides Are Mirror Images of Each Other

Figure 9.9 Tiles Laid Down on a 7 × 10 Rectangular Shape

Don't Use Tiles to Figure Out the Perimeter

In teaching how to figure out the perimeter of a polygon, Jane divided her children into several groups and handed out to each group a rectangular piece of paper. She said, "What I've just given you is the floor plan of our room and let's see what its perimeter is. Here for each group is a bag of 'tiles'; each one represents a 1 meter by 1 meter square. First lay the tiles along the edge of the floor plan. Next count how many meters each side is and then sum up all the sides."

All the groups of children laid the tiles down as Jane had directed (see Figure 9.9). However, while some groups figured out the correct perimeter to be 34, a few others didn't. They simply counted all the tiles around the perimeter and figured it to be 30.

Figure 9.10 Matches Laid Around a 7 × 10 Rectangular Shape

You have probably noticed that the difference between the two measures is 4. That's exactly what the four tiles at the corners did: Each one covered 2 units on the perimeter but got counted just once.

A way to help children see the length of each side more clearly, you may want to use thin, long objects such as matches (with their heads removed). For the aforementioned activity, prepare pieces of paper with lengths of 7 matches × 10 matches. Then give each group enough matches, with each one representing 1 meter, and ask all groups to lay the matches around the paper passed out, as shown in Figure 9.10.

The key point in this latter type of modeling is that no units at the corner will get accidentally skipped. As indicated by Figure 9.10, the perimeter of that shape is 10 + 7 + 10 + 7 = 34 meters. And this is a good practice for introducing the upcoming formula for calculating the perimeter of rectangles: perimeter = 2 × length + 2 × width, or perimeter = 2 × (length + width).

10

Geometry: Common Geometric Shapes

Length Doesn't Necessarily Mean Longer

Jane drew a rectangle on the board and said this to her class: "What you see here is a rectangle. You've probably noticed the horizontal pair of sides are parallel and congruent, and the vertical pair of sides are also parallel and congruent. Let's first name these sides. The longer sides are called lengths, and the shorter sides are called widths."

Linguistically, true, the word *length* comes from *long*, and it makes sense to assume that "length" refers to the longer sides of a rectangle. But this assumption won't hold true if we use the same logic for width: "*Width* comes from *wide*, so the wider sides are called widths, and the narrower sides are called lengths."

If this isn't convincing enough, let's consider a pair of common antonyms: *old* and *young*. No one will have any problem in saying a man who's lived for 70 years is old and a baby who's lived for 7 days is young. However, when we describe their age, we use *old* in both cases: "The man over there is 70 years *old*" and "The baby over there is 7 days *old*." We don't say "The baby is 7 days *young*," although a 7-day-old (again, *old*) baby can hardly be said to be "old." The reason is this: When we aren't using *old* in comparison with *young*, but rather when we're using it to mean "age," it's an unmarked term and doesn't necessarily have to do with being old. The same is true with *length*. When we use it to refer to a side, it doesn't necessarily have to be longer than the other sides. It can be shorter than the other sides, but still we call it *length*.

Simply put, when a term is used in an academic discipline such as mathematics, this term usually has its own specific meaning, and this meaning can be different from its everyday usage, just as *child* for tax filing purposes has specific definitions and may be different from what we usually use it to refer to.

So, what's the mathematical difference between *length* and *width*? None. In a rectangle where the two pairs of sides are different in their linear distances (I've intentionally avoided using *length* here), length is one dimension and width is the other. It really *doesn't* matter one way or the other. It doesn't make any difference either. For example, suppose the longer side of a rectangle is 8 centimeters and the shorter side is 5 centimeters. If we name the longer side "length" ($l = 8$) and the shorter side "width" ($w = 5$), then the perimeter of this rectangle is $p = 2l + 2w = 2 \times 8 + 2 \times 5 = 16 + 10 = 26$ cm, and its area is $a = lw = 8 \times 5 = 40$ cm^2. Alternatively, if we name the shorter side length ($l = 5$) and the longer side width ($w = 8$), then the perimeter is $p = 2l + 2w = 2 \times 5 + 2 \times 8 = 10 + 16 = 26$ cm, and its area is $a = lw = 5 \times 8 = 40$ cm^2. Not a thing has come up differently.

A look at this problem in a different perspective will tell us why it shouldn't matter one way or the other. Suppose there were such a stipulation that the longer sides were called "lengths" and the shorter sides "widths." How could we accommodate a square? We know a square is a special rectangle and—while it has its own perimeter and area formulas for easier calculation purposes ($p = 4s$ and $a = s^2$, where s refers to the side)—any formula for a rectangle should apply to a square as well. For example, if a square has a side of 5 cm (see Figure 10.1), then its perimeter and area are $p = 4s = 4 \times 5 = 20$ cm and $a = s^2 = 5^2 = 25$ cm^2. Then, by way of formulas for a rectangle, $p = 2l + 2w = 2 \times 5 + 2 \times 5 = 10 + 10 = 20$ cm and $a = lw = 5 \times 5 = 25$ cm^2 (in any square, $l = w = s$), respectively. This should hardly come as a surprise, because if formulas for rectangles didn't apply to squares, then squares would no longer

Figure 10.1 A 5 × 5 Square

The perimeter and area of a square can be calculated using the formulas for a rectangle because it is a rectangle.

be rectangles. If lengths must be longer than widths, how can anybody ever be able to decide which pair is the lengths and which pair is the widths since they happen to be equivalent?

To use an actual example: If a person's computer screen is 20 cm from top to bottom (shorter) but 30 cm from left to right (longer), then is that person wrong to say that the width of the computer's screen is 30 cm, if you think that *width* is the shorter side of a rectangle?

In short, the *length* of a rectangle can be either the longer *or* shorter side. And the same is true for *width*.

A Rectangle's Orientation Doesn't Matter Either

As *width* in its everyday use is usually defined as "distance from side to side," Jane told her children to distinguish it from *length* in this way: "Look at the rectangle in front of you. The two parallel sides that go up and down are called *lengths*. The two that go from side to side are called *widths*."

Just as it doesn't matter whether the longer sides or the shorter ones of a rectangle are called "lengths," its orientation, or layout, doesn't matter either. Coupled with the situation where one pair of sides are longer than the other, there are two scenarios to consider. The layout may resemble a door, or it may resemble a television screen. For both scenarios, the length can be the vertical distance and the width the other dimension, or the length can be the horizontal distance and the width the other dimension. It doesn't matter at all which way you call it.

Let's see why it should *not* matter one way or the other. Suppose we specify that the dimension from left to right was width and the dimension from top to bottom was length: What about a rectangle tilted 45° when neither pair of sides were strictly horizontal or vertical (see Figure 10.2). Now which is which? Should we say that we can't handle such a rectangle any longer?

Figure 10.2 A Tilted Rectangle

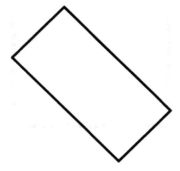

The confusion is even worse if the layout and the lengths of the two pairs of sides are combined. Suppose it was stipulated that the longer side was length and the shorter side was width, and further suppose it was stipulated that the side from left to right was the width and the side from top to bottom is the length. Then how can we deal with a rectangle whose longer side is from left to right, such as a television screen? Now children can really get confused.

Simply put, the *width* of a rectangle can run from left to right *or* from top to bottom or whatever direction if the figure is tilted—and the same is true for *length*.

"A Rectangle Has Two Longer Sides and Two Shorter Sides"

In comparing a rectangle to a square, Jane said this to her children: "A square has four congruent sides but a rectangle has two longer sides and two shorter sides." Before we take on this issue, let's start with the defining features of each shape, as listed in the following Math in Action boxes.

> ☑ **Math in Action: Defining Features of a Rectangle**
>
> - Quadrilateral (four-sided);
> - opposite sides parallel to each other;
> - *opposite sides congruent* (equal in length); and
> - all four angles are right angles.

> ☑ **Math in Action: Defining Features of a Square**
>
> - Quadrilateral;
> - opposite sides parallel to each other;
> - *all four sides congruent*; and
> - all four angles are right angles.

Here, all the features for both shapes are identical except for one: For a rectangle, the opposite sides are congruent whereas for a square, all four sides are congruent (this feature is italicized in the boxes).

Let's take up the rectangle first. For any rectangle, each pair of opposite sides are congruent. There are two possibilities concerning the relationship between these two pairs: One possibility is that one pair is longer than the other, and the other possibility is one pair is as long as the other. Since the

Figure 10.3 An Illustration of the Relationship Between Rectangles and Squares

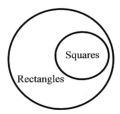

defining features of a rectangle don't say anything concerning the relationship between these two pairs of sides, we have to assume that whether one pair of sides is longer than the other pair, or one pair is as long as the other, is irrelevant to whether a shape is a rectangle or not.

Let's use a concrete case to explain this. Suppose we take a 10 cm × 6 cm rectangle and then increase the shorter sides by an increment of 1 cm. Its measurement will be 10 × 7, 10 × 8, 10 × 9, and so on. By the defining features of a rectangle, as long as the opposite sides of this shape are congruent and parallel and the angles are right angles, it remains a rectangle. Because we're increasing the two shorter sides at the same time, none of the defining features is being altered, and we have to conclude that what we have after each increase remains a rectangle.

When the shorter sides of this figure have been increased to the point where they are of the same length with the original longer sides, the measurement is now 10 × 10. This shape doesn't cease to be a rectangle simply because the two pairs of sides happen to be congruent. In other words, their being congruent doesn't disqualify such a shape from being a rectangle. No definition of the rectangle ever says that the two pairs of opposite sides must be of different lengths in order to be a rectangle. When they are of the same length, it's still a rectangle: It's simply a special rectangle. We call this special rectangle a square.

The relationship between rectangles and squares can be illustrated with the diagram in Figure 10.3.

This diagram indicates that the relationship between these two categories is such that one is a subset of the other. They aren't mutually exclusive of each other. Specifically, all squares are rectangles, but not all rectangles are squares. A squares is just a special kind of rectangle.

What's Wrong with Saying "Triangles, Rectangles, Squares, and Hexagons"?

Although Jane realized that a square is a special rectangle, in practice she often regarded these two shapes, unwittingly, as being two different categories. For example, before presenting geometric solids, Jane wanted her

Figure 10.4 Geometric Shapes That Aren't Mutually Exclusive of Each Other

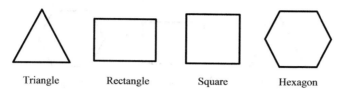

Triangle   Rectangle   Square   Hexagon

children to review some common 2-D shapes so that when it came to a face on a solid, they could easily recognize that shape. She drew several figures on the board (see Figure 10.4) and said, "We have learned different two-dimensional shapes such as triangles, rectangles, squares, and hexagons, and now we are going to move on to three-dimensional shapes."

The mistake here is juxtaposing rectangles and squares, and giving children the impression that each type of shape is independent of the other. In fact, this is the root for the common misconception that a rectangle has two longer sides and two shorter sides, as discussed in the previous section.

When a list of things is enumerated, each member is usually independent of any other member in the list. In other words, they should be mutually exclusive of each other. You may say to your children, for example, "Please take out a pencil, a marker, and a piece of paper." But you probably won't say "Please take out a pencil, a marker, and a red marker", because *a marker* and *a red marker* are not mutually exclusive of each other: A red marker is still a marker. If your children are old enough, they may even ask, "Isn't a red marker also a marker?"

Similarly, it's problematic to say "triangles, rectangles, squares, and hexagons" because the members here aren't mutually exclusive of each other. It's as if you were saying "a pencil, a marker, and a red marker"—and decide for yourself if you don't have any problem saying "Triangles, equilateral triangles, and rectangles."

The reason that many people wouldn't juxtapose "a marker and a red marker," or "a triangle and an equilateral triangle" but would often juxtapose "a rectangle and a square" is that the words *rectangle* and *square* don't share anything in common as *marker* and *red marker* do. That *rectangle* and *square* are totally different words leads to the misconception that they are mutually exclusive figures, and to rationalize this misconception some people created this "feature" for rectangles: "A rectangle has two longer sides and two shorter sides." This is the same mistake as thinking that a marker can't be a red marker at the same time.

Back to the example at the beginning of this section about reviewing a list of common geometric shapes, Jane can avoid making this mistake by simply

Figure 10.5 Geometric Shapes That Are Mutually Exclusive of Each Other

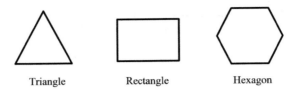

listing "Triangles, rectangles, and hexagons" (see Figure 10.5). Should a child mention "squares," she may say something to the effect of "Squares are just a type of rectangles" or "Rectangles include squares."

Because the words *rectangle* and *square* have no linguistic linkage to each other, causing many children to believe that they represent mutually exclusive figures, a better way to handle this would be to avoid saying *square* altogether. When there is need to refer to such a shape, *equilateral rectangle* will do the job nicely. There are several reasons for this recommendation. First, a rectangle is to a square what a triangle is to an equilateral triangle. Due to the linguistic linkage between *a triangle* and *an equilateral triangle*, the relation between the two is self-evident (equilateral triangles are a subset of triangles, triangles subsume equilateral triangles, all equilateral triangles are still triangles, etc.). Children usually don't have any difficulty distinguishing two categories of objects with one type having a name composed of the other plus a modifier. By the same token, if a square is referred to as *an equilateral rectangle*, it is as clear as *equilateral triangle* is. Children will easily perceive *an equilateral rectangle* as a subset of rectangles, and they will have no trouble understanding that an equilateral rectangle is still a rectangle.

Second, it will be no longer necessary for teachers to spend much time explaining the relationship between these two terms—no more clichés like "All squares are rectangles but not all rectangles are squares."

Third, and most importantly, there will be no such mistakes as enumerating non-mutually exclusive things like "triangles, rectangles, squares, and hexagons." When squares are referred to as equilateral rectangles, it will be as unlikely for teachers and their children to say "triangles, rectangles, and equilateral rectangles" as to say "Please take out a pencil, a marker, and a red marker."

Base Doesn't Necessarily Mean "Side at Bottom"

Jane drew a triangle on the board as indicated by Figure 10.6 and told her class, "In order to find the area of a triangle, we need to know its base and height. The base of a triangle is the side at the bottom. Let's label it *b*. The

Figure 10.6 A Triangle With the Horizontal Side at the Bottom

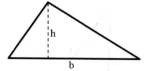

Figure 10.7 A Triangle With the Horizontal Side at the Top

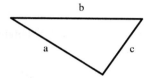

height is the perpendicular distance between the base and its opposite vertex. Let's label it *h*."

But Jane soon found herself in an awkward situation when a child approached her and, presenting her with a figure where the horizontal side was at the top rather than at the bottom (see Figure 10.7), asked, "What is the base of this triangle when the horizontal side is at the top?"

Can a side other than the one at the bottom be called a base, such as the top side in Figure 10.7? More importantly, can the formula for the area of a triangle still be applicable if the given side is at the top, instead at the bottom, as side *b* shown in Figure 10.7? Undoubtedly, the answer to both questions is "yes."

Misunderstanding the term *base* for meaning the side at the bottom perhaps stems from the root meaning of the word: "the bottom of something." When the term was first decided on, mathematicians probably had the side at the bottom in mind (*Longman Dictionary of Contemporary English* defines *base* as "a line on which a figure stands"). But when a term is used in describing something in a specific discipline such as mathematics, the meaning associated with the discipline can be different from its everyday meaning or usage, as we discussed earlier in this chapter. *Base* is just one such term.

Concerning the specific problem at hand, the layout of a triangle really doesn't matter with regard to its perimeter or area. For example, we can simply rotate the triangle as shown in Figure 10.6 into different orientations (see Figures 10.8 and 10.9) and, with the same given measures, the resulting area will not be affected at all.

So, you may ask, how should I define the base of a triangle? Since the layout doesn't matter at all, you may simply say "The base of a triangle is any one of its three sides." In Figure 10.7 shown above, either *a*, *b*, or *c* can be the base of that triangle.

Figure 10.8 The Triangle in Figure 10.6 Has Been Rotated, With Its Base on the Upper Right Side

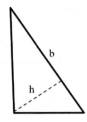

Figure 10.9 The Triangle in Figure 10.6 Has Been Further Rotated, With Its Base on the Upper Left Side

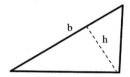

It is worth noting, however, that once the base has been designated, the height must be defined in relation to this base so that the formula $area = \frac{1}{2} \cdot base \cdot height$ can be used to find the area. More specifically, the height is the perpendicular distance between this base and the opposite vertex. This is similar to the case of the area formula for a rectangle, expressed as *area = length · width*. As mentioned earlier in this chapter, the length can be any one of the four sides. But after the length has been designated, either one of the two sides perpendicular to the length is to be regarded as the width of the rectangle.

Three Sides Don't Necessarily Make a Triangle

After giving her children the definition of the perimeter of a polygon, Jane started with the polygon of the fewest sides: the triangle. She told them that to find the perimeter of a triangle, what they needed to do was add up the lengths of its three sides. For practice, she listed a few triangles, each with three numbers indicating the lengths of its three sides. For the last triangle, she said, "This triangle has three sides with lengths of 7, 13, and 5 centimeters. What's its perimeter?"

Few people would make a mistake on the sum of the three angle measures of a triangle. For example, if one of Jane's children said to her that he had a triangle with angle measures of 50°, 50°, and 90°, Jane would immediately tell him that it's impossible to have such a triangle because in plane geometry, the sum of the three angle measures in any triangle is always 180°. But Jane was not aware that there is a restriction on the lengths of a triangle's three sides as well, as expressed in the triangle inequality theorem. Simply put, this theorem states that in any triangle, the sum of any two sides is greater than the third. Conversely, any one side of a triangle is shorter than the sum of the two other sides. Applied to a daily-life situation, this theorem can explain why a shortcut is shorter. Suppose you are at point A going to point C through point B, as shown in Figure 10.10, you will find going from A to C directly through the lawn is shorter—because the shortcut involves one side of this triangle whereas going from A to B and then to C involves the sum of the other two sides.

Jane's mistake of enumerating the lengths of the three sides of a triangle as being 7, 13, and 5 centimeters would immediately become apparent if she attempted to draw such a triangle to scale. We can make this attempt for her here. Let's designate the three sides having lengths of 7, 13, and 5 centimeters as sides a, b, and c, respectively. First, using actual measures, let's draw side b (13 cm, the longest side) on a piece of graph paper. At one endpoint of side b let's draw side a (7 cm) as close to it as possible. Next, at the other endpoint of b, let's draw side c (5 cm), also as close to it as possible (see Figure 10.11). We can easily see that no matter how close sides a and c are to side b, their endpoints won't join each other to make a triangle. In other words, a and c added together must be longer than b in order for all three sides to join each other to make a triangle. This is what the triangle inequality theorem is about.

To avoid making similar mistakes, you may want to do one of two things. First, after you have come up with the lengths of the three sides of a triangle,

Figure 10.10 Going From A to C Directly (the Shortcut) Is Shorter Than Going From A to C Through B Because the Shortcut Involves One Side of This Triangle Whereas Going From A to B and Then to C Involves the Sum of the Other Two Sides

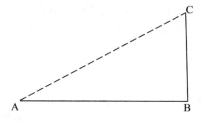

Figure 10.11 There Is No Way to Make a Triangle With Three Lengths of 7, 13, and 5 Centimeters

try to draw this triangle to scale. If the triangle inequality theorem is violated, you won't be able to accomplish drawing such a triangle, just as it happened when we were trying to draw the triangle with sides of 7, 13, and 5 centimeters. The second method may be easier. Simply rearrange the three lengths in order from longest to shortest. Then add up the two shortest sides. If the sum is not longer than the longest side, they won't make a triangle. For example, for the three lengths mentioned earlier, rearrange them into 13, 7, and 5. The sum of 7 and 5 is not greater than 13, so they won't make a triangle.

How Many Sides Does a Circle Have?

After teaching triangles, rectangles, and hexagons, Jane moved on to circles. Wanting to make a connection to the shapes her children had already learned, Jane brought up the number of sides a shape has as a starting point. She said, "A triangle has three sides, a rectangle has four sides, a pentagon has five sides, and so on. But a circle has zero sides."

To investigate this issue, let's start with polygons. By definition, a *polygon* is a simple closed figure composed of three or more line segments joined at their endpoints. These line segments are called the polygon's sides. Some polygons have special names with a Greek root referring to the number of sides they have (*-gon* actually means "angles"), such as pentagon (*penta-* means "five"), hexagon (*hexa-* means "six"), and heptagon (*hepta-* means "seven").

A circle, in contrast, is *not* composed of line segments (sides) as a polygon is, and thus it doesn't fall in the family of polygons. So "the number of sides a circle has" is in itself a pseudo-proposition, because *side* is not a feature attributed to circles. We can use the number of bones in mammals as an example to illustrate this.

People sometimes use the number of bones to describe a group in Kingdom Animalia, such as "A human being has 206 bones" and "A cat has 290 bones." But we don't use the number of bones to describe anything in Kingdom Plantae, as bones don't exist in it. Thus, asking how many sides a circle has is like asking "How many bones does a tree have?", and saying that a circle has 0 sides is like saying "A tree has no bones." In other words, although it isn't technically wrong to say "A circle has 0 sides", this statement in itself isn't very rigorous or proper.

Meanwhile, several other statements concerning the number of sides a circle has can be considered wrong, such as "A circle has 1 side" and "A circle has infinitely many sides."

11

Time-Telling

"A Quarter in Time Means 15"

Jane was teaching her children different units of time and how to tell time from an analog clock. Knowing that they had knowledge of money due to hearing and saying *quarter* on a daily basis, she wanted them to distinguish between a quarter used in money and a quarter used in time. So she started her lesson saying, "A quarter in money means 25, but a quarter in time means 15."

There're in fact two mistakes here.

First, a quarter, when written out as a number, is a constant, and its value doesn't change. The way Jane said it leaves her children the impression that this number adopts different values when used with different entities.

Second, a quarter doesn't mean either 25 or 15. A quarter is a fraction, namely, one fourth (1/4). When used as a money unit, it means one fourth of a dollar. As a dollar is customarily divided into 100 cents, a quarter of a dollar is 1/4 of 100 cents, which is 25 cents. There's a coin for this unit of money: a quarter of a dollar. This coin is commonly referred to as a "quarter." When people say *quarter* in this sense, it's the coin name that is intended, just like a *dime* or *nickel*, rather than the numerical meaning.

When *quarter* is used to measure time, it's still 1/4, only it's 1/4 of an hour. Since an hour is 60 minutes, 1/4 of 60 minutes is 15 minutes. Does *quarter* have a changed meaning here? No, it still means 1/4.

The confusion lies in the fact that *quarter*, as a coin name, has come to be associated with 25 cents for many children. In contrast, even though there's a coin with a name similarly composed of a fraction—the half-dollar coin—the word *half* hasn't gained the status of the name of the coin (possibly because half-dollar coins aren't nearly as omnipresent as quarters are). In daily life people may say "All I have on me is a quarter" but never say "All I have on me is a half." Instead, they may say "All I have on me is a half-dollar coin." Because of this, children usually don't associate *half* with 50 cents.

Depending on the different entities used with *quarter,* it may be 1/4 of a dollar, 1/4 of an hour, or 1/4 of whatever we want to measure. For example, a full NBA game is divided into four parts, with each part being (naturally) a quarter. As a full game is 48 minutes, here a quarter is 1/4 of 48 minutes, which is 12 minutes. But a full NCAA game is 40 minutes, so a quarter of an NCAA game is 10 minutes. Some other examples include "a quarter inch," "a quarter mile," and so on. Even in the realm of time, *quarter* can be used with other units as well, such as 1/4 of a year, as in "Sales went up in the second quarter of this year." In any case, a quarter is 1/4, and is neither 25, nor 15, nor any other number of whatever it happens to be used to measure.

Does 1 on Analog Clocks Mean 5 Minutes?

When it came to telling the number of hours and number of minutes on an analog clock, Jane told her children how to produce the two numbers in this way: "When you want to tell the number of hours, say the number the hour hand points to as it is. But when you want to tell the number of minutes, you look at the number the minute hand points to, and then multiply it by 5. So, when you see 1, it's 5 minutes, when you see 2, it's 10 minutes, when you see 3, it's 15 minutes, and so on."

What Jane said here isn't a conceptually rigorous way of teaching children how to tell hours and minutes. What if the minute hand points to somewhere between 1 and 2? Should we tell them to do $1.5 \times 5 = 7.5$? This isn't an appropriate option for elementary school children. Of course Jane might argue that, by her reasoning, when the minute hand is pointing at the midpoint between 1 and 2, the number of minutes should be halfway between 5 and 10, which is 7.5 minutes.

Jane has, actually, been deceived by the large, visually salient numbers on the clock face. Those numbers, 1–12, are for the hours only. There's another set of numbers, 1–60, for the minutes, right outside the first set of numbers. But these 60 numbers have to be very small to be printed on the outer ring of the clock face, and in many cases they don't fit—and even if they do, they are often left off because they wouldn't look very appealing. Manufacturers handle this problem in several different ways. They may print 60 short bars

Figure 11.1 On This Clock Face, 60 Bars Are Printed for the Minute Hand, With Only Every Fifth Number Printed

for the minute hand, with only every fifth bar accompanied by its corresponding number (5, 10, 15, etc.). Sometimes they may print these multiple-of-5 numbers on the inner circle to take advantage of the space there, as shown in Figure 11.1. Or they may print all 60 bars, with every fifth bar thicker or longer, without actually printing any numbers (see Figure 11.2). This design is the most common. Some clocks don't have either numbers or marks for the minutes at all (see Figure 11.3). Such a design is not good for teaching time to elementary school children.

The point here is, there's one set of numbers for the hour hand and a different set of numbers for the minute hand, and children should know which set of numbers is for which hand. They need to be taught that in order to tell the number of hours, they should read the larger set of numbers on the inner circle, which the tip of the hour hand falls on. When they want to tell the number of minutes, they should use the small marks or bars (sometimes with every fifth number printed or every fifth mark made thicker) on the outer circle. They are most likely on the outer circle because the minute hand is longer, and that's where its tip falls. Adults often don't even bother to look at

Figure 11.2 On This Clock Face, no Numbers Are Printed for the Minute Hand; Every Fifth Mark Is Thicker

Figure 11.3 On This Clock Face, no Numbers or Marks for the Minute Hand Are Printed

these small marks. But for children, it's important that they distinguish these two sets of numbers.

In this sense, it's conceptually wrong to say "When the minute hand is on 6, it is 30 minutes past the hour." That 6 belongs with the set of numbers for hours.

"Why Does the Time on My Analog Clock Look Weird?"

Jane has a model analog clock in her classroom that allows her to move its two hands freely and demonstrate whatever time she wants to show to her children. During her lesson on how to tell time, Jane wrote "9:30" on the board and said, "It's 9:30 now and let's see how we can make our clock show this time. First, we need to put the hour hand on the bigger number 9, which means the number of hours. Then we need to point the minute hand to the outside, smaller number 30, which means the number of minutes." Figure 11.4 shows what Jane's clock looks like for 9:30 (Figure 11.4).

Then Jane found that her clock looked weird but didn't know why. Let's figure this out for her.

Have you observed the movement of the hour hand and minute hand of a real analog clock or a mechanical watch? Suppose you have one in front of you; let's go over the movement. At 9:00, the hour hand points to 9 even, and

Figure 11.4 A Wrong Layout of Hands for 9:30

Figure 11.5 The Correct Layout of Hands for 9:30

the minute hand points to 0 (some clocks have 60 printed on them, which, strictly speaking, is wrong). As the minute hand moves forward, the hour hand doesn't sit there idly: It also moves forward, although at a much slower rate. After the minute hand has completed a full circle and arrived at 0 again, the hour hand has edged forward for 1/12 of a circle, and it is pointing to 10 now. Halfway during this process, at 9:30, the minute hand has completed half of the circle and should be pointing to 30 minutes. Where should the hour hand be pointing to now? Again, it hasn't remained immobile at 9. It's been moving. It's left 9 but hasn't reached 10 yet: It's halfway between 9 and 10. A clock showing this time should look like Figure 11.5.

A similar mistake under a different disguise may also be very common. For example, Jane asked her children to demonstrate 6:15. After she had them put the minute hand at 15 minutes, she asked, "Is the hour hand on 6 or 7?" She was expecting to hear "6," so then she put the hour hand on 6. However, although it's wrong to put the hour hand on 7, it's not right to put it on 6 either. Theoretically, unless the time is exactly 6:00 where the hour hand is on 6, and unless it's exactly 7:00 where the hour hand is on 7, any time between these two points will cause the hour hand to be away from landing exactly on either 6 or 7. Of course sometimes the distance the hour hand has traveled is so small that even if it's put on the even hour it may not be noticeable. For example, if the minute hand has traveled for 5 minutes after 6:00 (6:05) and we still put the hour hand on exactly 6, it will be hardly noticeable to most people. However, that doesn't mean that the small distance should be disregarded.

The whole idea is that the hour hand doesn't "jump" from 6 to 7 at one single moment and then stays immobile for the next full hour. It's moving gradually but continuously. Exactly how far it's away from the previous whole hour is a function of the number of minutes that has passed in relation to the whole hour. When the minute hand has moved for a fourth of an hour, the hour hand should also have moved for a fourth of an hour, too. The only difference is that the minute hand has moved for a fourth of a full circle (which is 1 hour) while the hour hand has moved for a fourth of the distance between 6 and 7 on the clock (which is also 1 hour).

For this reason, it's a good idea to choose model analog clocks that have coordinated hands. In other words, to set a time on such a clock, all a child has to do is turn the minute hand only. Then the hour hand will be moved by the wheels behind the clock face to its correct position.

Which Hand Pointing to 12 Makes 12:00?

As 12:00 noon is the dividing time between morning and afternoon hours and at this time the two hands on an analog clock point directly upward, Jane chose this time to teach her children how to tell the whole hour. She set her clock at this time, wrote 12:00 on the board, and told her class that the time her clock was showing was 12 o'clock.

But this is the hour that Jane should, by all means, avoid using in teaching how to tell the whole hour. Let's see why.

Suppose a high school student from a foreign country came to stay with you as an exchange student. In her home country, all clocks are digital, and this student had never seen an analog clock before. Now you wanted to show her how to tell time on an analog clock. You demonstrated with your clock, saying, "Now let me make the hour hand point to 3 and the minute hand point to 12 and this is 3:00."[1] Then you continued, "I'll go get something to drink. When I'm back, you show me what the clock is like for 5:00." Then you left the room.

The young woman reasoned, "The shorter hand pointing to 3 and the longer hand pointing to 12 makes 3:00. If I want to make 5:00, I can simply make the shorter hand point to 5 without changing anything else." When you came back, she showed you the time and it was right.

Now let's consider a different scenario. If, instead of 3:00, you showed her 12:00 and asked her to show you 5:00. Again, let's trace her mind work to see how she would accomplish this task. She thought, "Both the longer hand and shorter hand pointing to 12 makes 12:00. Now I want to make 5:00. Do I make both hands point to 5? Or should I move the longer hand to 5 while leaving the shorter hand at 12? Or should I move the shorter hand to 5 and leave the long hand at 12?" With only the example of 12:00 given, there was no way for her to know exactly how to show 5:00. In other words, the example of 12:00 did not help at all.

Children starting to learn how to tell time on an analog clock are just like this exchange student. This is why 12:00 should be avoided as an example to show children how to tell the whole hour at the beginning stage, because after this example, they still don't know which hand pointing to 12 makes 12:00. Any other hour will work well, be it 3:00, 5:00, or 10:00.

Why We Shouldn't Jump Around Between 8:00 and 9:00

After she felt that her children could tell whole and half hours on an analog clock, Jane began to throw in times at 5-minute intervals. With a model clock, she showed different times, making sure that the number of minutes is a multiple of 5, and asked her children to say out loud: 4:20, 7:55, 1:10, 8:50, and so on. But she soon found that her children were sometimes off on the number for hours, such as saying 9:50 instead of 8:50 for the time indicated by the clock in Figure 11.6. The reason is that the hour hand in this example was much closer to 9 than it was to 8.

Figure 11.6 Children Often Say That the Time on This Clock Is 9:50

Figure 11.7 From 8:00 (a) to 9:00 (b), the Minute Hand Turns One Full Circle While the Hour Hand Turns Only 1/12 of That Angle

(a)   (b)

As mentioned earlier in this chapter, the hour hand on an analog clock moves as the minute hand does, but at a much slower rate. To be exact, for every full circle (360°) the minute hand moves, the hour hand moves only 1/12 of that angle. For example, for a full hour between 8:00 and 9:00, the minute hand will make a complete turn, from the original upright position and back at that position again, but the hour hand will move only 1/12 of that angle, with it originally pointing to 8 now pointing to 9 (see Figure 11.7).

For the first half hour after 8:00, the hour hand is closer to 7 than is to 8, and most children will have little trouble telling the correct hour. For example, most children will be able to tell the time represented by Figure 11.8 to be 8:15.

Things will be different for the second half hour, that is, after 8:30. At 8:50, for example, the hour hand is much closer to 9 than is to 8 (see Figure 11.6). That is why Jane's children made the mistake of saying that it was 9:50 instead of 8:50.

Now probably you can see Jane's mistake of having her children learn how to tell the second half hour at the same time of how to tell the first half. Given that the second half hour can cause confusion at the beginning, it will be a good idea for Jane to have her children practice the first half extensively before moving on to the second. After they become comfortable telling the first half, Jane would need to *gradually* move to the first few minutes after the half hour mark. For example, suppose Jane sets the clock at 8:30 and her children can tell it correctly. If she says she is going to show 5 minutes after that and then moves the clock to 8:35, it is likely that many of them will say that it's 8:35 because they hear her say it's 5 minutes after 8:30 and they see her move the clock 5 minutes after the previous time. If Jane keeps moving

Figure 11.8 Most Children Have no Difficulty Telling This Time

Figure 11.9 A Point May Be Closer to 40 Than It Is to 30 on a Number Line, yet Until We Reach 40, We Say "Thirty-Something"

the clock in this gradual manner, her children will probably follow the pattern of saying 8:35, 8:40, 8:45, 8:50, and 8:55. Then, at this moment, Jane will need to help her children arrive at the conclusion that the number of hours is determined by the number the hour hand has *passed* and *left behind*, not the number it's closer to. In other words, as long as the hour hand hasn't reached the next hour, it's still the previous hour that should be called out, no matter how close it is to the next hour.

In addition, Jane could try to use the number line as an analogy (see Figure 11.9). A point after 35 on a number line—say, 38, is closer to 40 than it is to 30. However, we don't say 48. No matter how close to 40 we are as we move towards it, we keep using 30s, such as 37, 38, 39, until we reach 40.

Note

1 Actually, it should be 0 (or 60 on some clocks) rather than 12 because this is the number for the minutes (see "Does 1 on Analog Clocks Mean 5 Minutes" in this chapter). Here 12 is used to follow the same misconception of using the hour number for minutes.

12

Fractions

A Condition for Using Fractions: Equivalent Parts

Jane told her children that they were going to learn fractions, and they were excited. To start with, she drew a circle on the board, then drew three vertical bars on it dividing the circle into four parts, and said, "A fraction expresses parts of a whole. We just divided this circle into four parts. If we take one part, that's 1 of 4." (see Figure 12.1).

Jane's definition of a fraction, that it expresses parts of a whole, was correct. But this definition has a condition that needs to be satisfied: When we divide a whole thing into a number of parts, these parts have to be of equal

Figure 12.1 A Circle Divided Into 4 Unequal Parts

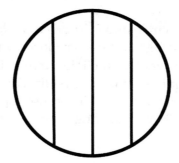

Figure 12.2 A Circle Divided Into 2 (a), 4 (b), and 8 (c) Equivalent Parts

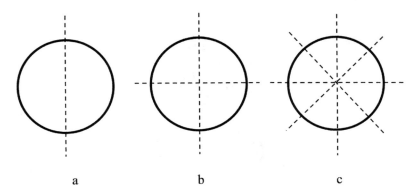

size to be expressed with a fraction. Otherwise, the fraction may not be a correct representation of the parts in relation to the whole. In the figure Jane drew (Figure 12.1), the two pieces in the middle were larger than the two pieces on the outer sections.

We may make an analogy to multiplication being referred to as repeated addition, in which case each set should consist of the same number of elements as any other set. Suppose Jane bought 8 packs of pencils and each pack contained 12. Jane could use multiplication to find out the total number of pencils she had bought: $8 \times 12 = 96$. However, suppose Jane bought 8 packs of pencils, but some packs contained 12 pencils each, some other packs contained 10 each, and still others contained 6 each. In this case she may not use $8 \times$ ___ to solve this problem because not all packs contained the same number of pencils.

A way to modify Jane's picture so that a fraction may be used to express one or more parts of it is to draw lines that pass through the center of the circle. If you want to divide a circle into 2, 4, or 8 equivalent parts, you can simply fold the circle 1, 2, or 3 times, respectively, and use the creases as dividing lines (see Figure 12.2).

If you want to divide a circle into 3, 5 or 6 equivalent parts, you can divide each of these numbers into 360° and use a protractor to measure out the angle of each of the sections you want your circle cut into. For example, if you want to divide a circle into 5 equivalent parts, first find out the angle measurement of each of the sections: $360° \div 5 = 72°$. Then use a protractor to divide your circle into five sections, with each having a central angle measurement of $72°$ (see Figure 12.3).

Figure 12.3 A Circle Divided Into 5 Equivalent Parts

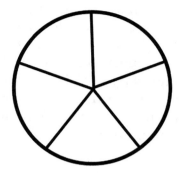

"Bottom Number" and "Top Number" Aren't Nearly Sufficient for Defining Denominators and Numerators

Jane felt that her children had been given enough background information about fractions and decided to introduce to them the definition of the two key terms involving this concept: *denominator* and *numerator*. She said, "So what's the denominator? And what's the numerator? The denominator is the bottom number, and the numerator is the top number."

Such definitions aren't nearly sufficient for defining the two key components of a fraction. Let's put ourselves in the shoes of Jane's children to see why.

Suppose after giving the "denominator is the bottom number, and numerator is the top number" definition to her children, Jane assigned them this problem and asked them to write a fraction for what's expressed in the problem: "Megan's mom just baked a pizza. She cut it into 4 equal slices. Megan ate 1 slice. Write a fraction to express the portion of pizza that Megan ate."

With her definition, her children were still unable to handle this task. They might be wondering, "Which number should be my bottom number? And which number should be my top number?" This is because Jane's definition merely specifies the *position* of the two components but doesn't say anything about their *meaning* at all. Naturally, without knowing their meaning, her children couldn't tell which should be written as the bottom number and which should be written as the top number, as meaning is what bridges the original situation and a fraction that expresses it.

To give her children the proper concept of these two terms, Jane would need to tell them their meanings in addition to their positions. The "parts-of-a-whole" definition is a classic textbook definition and can be readily used with children here: "The denominator tells us how many equal parts a whole thing is divided into. The numerator tells us how many of these divided parts we are talking about." Of course, we have to follow this definition by where to write each of the two components: "We write the denominator under the fraction bar, and we write the numerator above the fraction bar."

Armed with this definition, Jane's children would be able to transcribe the situation presented earlier into a fraction. Let's trace their mind and see how it works. The text presented in the following Math in Action box shows how one fictitious child solves this problem.

> ☑ **Math in Action: Possible Mind Work of Transcribing the Pizza Situation**
>
> Ms. Smith just said the denominator is the number of equal parts a whole thing is divided into. Megan's mom cut her pizza into 4 equal slices. Then 4 must be the denominator. Megan ate 1 slice. This 1 slice is what we are talking about, so it should be the numerator. Next, since the denominator appears under the fraction bar, I need to write the 4 here, like this: $\frac{}{4}$. The numerator goes above it, so it should look like this: $\frac{1}{4}$.

Incidentally, it's always a good idea to define the denominator first, as it's the foundation for expressing a fraction. Without the denominator having been defined first, it's difficult to say what a numerator is. As an example, if you are given a fraction and told what the denominator is, such as 4, without being told what the numerator is, you could still possibly picture a situation as shown in Figure 12.2(b). In contrast, if you are told that the numerator of a fraction is 4 without being told what the denominator is, it's very difficult to picture anything in the mind.

What Does 1/2*x* Mean?

After Jane had her children represent a fraction using circular cutouts as pizzas, Jane came up with another idea. She gave each child a Hershey's chocolate bar and told them that they were going to use it to represent a fraction. She started by showing a whole chocolate bar, and then broke it into 12 equal pieces. She took one piece and said, "We broke this bar into 12 equal pieces. That's our denominator. This one piece is what I want to eat. So this is how we write this much using a fraction." She then wrote 1/12 on the board.

This written form, the slash in place of a horizontal fraction bar, isn't very good. To further discuss this issue, we need to trace how each of the symbols came to be used.

When fractions started to be represented in writing, it was the dividend over the divisor (so it makes sense to read a fraction as one number "over" another in English, or one number "sur" another number in French), with a horizontal bar in between, as $\frac{1}{12}$. Problems came with the age of printing, when it was apparent that fractions were more difficult to typeset and required a larger line space. At the same time, fractions didn't look aesthetic, with a line containing a fraction jarringly wider than the other lines. Publishers began to favor the solidus during the 19th century, as in $\frac{1}{12}$. With the solidus, the typesetting of fractions was easier, and the line space was not too much larger than a regular line. From the solidus, it was just a small step to move to the use of a forward slash on a typewriter or computer—because the solidus isn't available on the keyboard (the solidus is also called "diagonal," a 45-degree slanted line, whereas the slash on a typewriter or computer keyboard is more upright). Nowadays many people aren't even aware that a solidus and a slash are different characters.

It's apparent that using the forward slash is just the "computer" way, and a makeshift way at that, of substituting for a horizontal fraction bar. In an elementary classroom, most often teachers will have to handwrite fractions on the whiteboard and, likewise, students will handwrite fractions on their scratch paper. In such situations, there really is no reason to adopt this makeshift, computer way of using slashes in place of fraction bars. In other words, when a good symbol is readily available through handwriting, why settle for something less desirable?

You may ask, why is the slash a less desirable form to use for writing a fraction?

The main reason is, with a slash, the relation between the denominator and the numerator may be ambiguous. For example, $\frac{1}{2x}$ and $\frac{1}{2}x$ are totally different. However, if you type these two fractions on a computer using slashes, both expressions will end up being $1/2x$. In other words, it's difficult to tell whether the x in $1/2x$ belongs with the denominator or not. It often occurs that when students write down such fractions using slashes and are later asked about the relation among the terms, they can't remember themselves.

Unless the composition of a fraction is very simple, such as $1/2$, a slash can often be misleading. For example, suppose the expression $\frac{x+6}{x-1}$ is written with a slash, then two pairs of parentheses are needed so that its original meaning is preserved: (x + 6)/(x − 1). However, many children, and even some adults, aren't clear about when parentheses are necessary and when they're not, and may unwittingly omit them. When this happens, the value of this new fraction will not be the same as that of the original fraction. For the expression just mentioned, if it's written as x + 6/x − 1, then it means $x + \dfrac{6}{x} - 1$. This is quite different from the original $\dfrac{x+6}{x-1}$. You can test this out yourself. Give x + 6/x−1 to a group of high school students or even college students and ask them to evaluate it given x = 2, and you will likely get two different answers: 8 and 4.

Slashes aren't able to handle a fraction within a fraction, such as $\dfrac{\frac{2}{3}}{11}$ or $\dfrac{2}{\frac{3}{11}}$. The first expression has a value of $\dfrac{2}{33}$ whereas the second expression has a value of $\dfrac{22}{3}$. This is because division is not associative. In the first case $\dfrac{2}{3}$ is used as the numerator and 11 used as the denominator, and in the second case 2 is used as the numerator and $\dfrac{3}{11}$ used as the denominator. They have very different meanings. But when slashes are used, both expressions will be written as 2/3/11, and nobody can tell if the numerator has a fraction or the denominator has one.

An additional disadvantage of slashes is when you handle a series of fractions. For example, for the expression $\dfrac{5}{9} \times \dfrac{3}{4} \times \dfrac{6}{10} \times \dfrac{15}{8}$, regardless whether you simplify first and then multiply or multiply first and then simplify, the relationship among these numbers is clear. If you choose to simplify first, there are a number of different ways to do it because any denominator can be simplified with any numerator, such as the 9 in the first fraction simplified with 3, or with 6, or with 15. Not only that, you can keep simplifying until you can't simplify any further. For instance, after 9 is simplified into 3 with the 3 in the second fraction, it can be further simplified with the 6 in the third fraction. Since all denominators are below the central line (imagine drawing a line along all the four fraction bars) and all numerators are above the line, they can be easily distinguished. In contrast, if the above expression is written as 5/9 × 3/4 × 6/10 × 15/8, students have to be extremely careful when they simplify, because all numbers are in a roughly horizontal position, and they have to see if a number is before a slash or after it so as to determine if it's a denominator or numerator. It can be even more confusing if a number is simplified more than once.

For these reasons, cultivate in your children the habit of using horizontal bars in fractions.

A Fraction Doesn't Address "How Many"

To have her children make an easy connection with real things around them, Jane designed an activity where they were divided into several groups, with each group sitting around one table. She had each table group first count the total number of children in that group and then count how many of them were wearing sneakers. Then she asked, "How many children in your table group wear sneakers? Write a fraction on the card I gave you and hold it up when you finish." Jane walked around the room and checked on the results. There were 5 children at Table One, and two of them were wearing sneakers. They came up with $\frac{2}{5}$. At Table Two, all four children were wearing sneakers, and they were holding up a card saying $\frac{4}{4}$.

Although this activity was an engaging one and closely connected with the children's daily lives, the question Jane asked did not fit the answer she was soliciting. For the question, "How many children at your table wear sneakers?" the correct answer for Table One would simply be 2. Similarly, the answer for Table Two would be 4. In contrast, when the children at Table Two came up with the answer of $\frac{4}{4}$, this had the effect of 1, which is not the number of children at that table who were wearing sneakers.

This boils down to the definition of fractions. Recall that a fraction expresses the relation of a part to the whole. In other words, a fraction does *not* address the question of "how many." Instead, it expresses a ratio. Here two quantities are at play, very much like, for example, a cookie recipe which requires 1 cup of water and 3 cups of flour. If you want to make twice as many cookies, you can use 2 cups of water and 6 cups of flour. Even though the quantity for each ingredient has changed, the ratio has remained the same, and it still meets the requirement of the recipe.

In contrast to this requirement, Jane's question "How many children at your table wear sneakers?" would elicit one quantity only, while the intention of her activity was to produce a ratio, that is, a relation between two quantities. Thus, the original question should be changed to fit the activity Jane designed. Considering that the word *ratio* may be a little difficult for children at this stage, Jane may ask the question along the line of "What part of your group wears sneakers?"

The following Math in Action box lists several situations where the questions asked are in effect "how many" oriented even though the original intention is for soliciting fractions. Each question is then reworded so as to suggest a ratio.

☑ **Math in Action: Situations where a Ratio Is Intended**

- "How can you express this red M&M as a fraction?" after Jane opened a bag of 12 M&Ms, of which one was red. This one red M&M is just one red M&M. This question can be reworded as, "What *portion* of this bag of M&Ms is red?" or "How much of this bag of M&Ms is red?"
- Similarly, "How do you express these green M&Ms in a fraction form?" should be reworded as "How much of your bag of M&Ms is green?" or "What portion of all M&Ms is green?"
- "Look at my whiteboard here. I have drawn a grid of 3 rows and 5 columns of squares. Let me shade the top 5 squares. Now, how many squares are unshaded? Write a fraction for them." This question should be reworded as "How much of the grid is unshaded? Write a fraction for it."

Denominators Should Be Substantially Different for Easy Comparison

After spending several days working with her children on how to compare fractions of like denominators such as $\frac{1}{3}$ and $\frac{2}{3}$, Jane felt confident that they were ready to move on. So she decided to present the topic of comparing fractions of like numerators but unlike denominators. She gave this scenario: "Your mom baked two exact pizzas. She cut the first pizza into 5 equal slices and the second one into 6 equal slices. You are really hungry and want to eat as much as you can. But Mom says you can eat either a slice from the first pizza or a slice from the second pizza." After demonstrating the problem by drawing two circles representing the pizzas with the intended pieces shaded (see Figure 12.4), Jane posed this question: "Which piece should you pick?"

Figure 12.4 Jane Was Comparing 1/5 (a) and 1/6 (b)

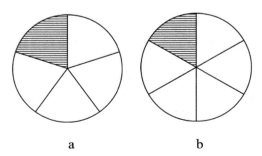

a   b

Children usually have no trouble comparing fractions of like denominators because, in such situations, the fraction with a larger numerator has a larger value. This is consistent with their prior knowledge on whole numbers. But the value scheme for fractions having like numerators but unlike denominators is just the opposite: a fraction with a larger denominator has a smaller value ($\frac{1}{6}$ is smaller than $\frac{1}{5}$). Many children at the beginning stage tend to pick $\frac{1}{6}$ as the larger fraction due to the influence of their prior knowledge on whole numbers (because 6 is greater than 5). Jane should be commended for making sure to present comparisons of fractions with like denominators first before taking up the current topic. She also did a good job coming up with a real-world situation that her children can make an easy connection to. Despite all this, they were still making frequent errors when comparing fractions having unlike denominators. Jane was wondering what would be a better way to handle this topic.

A brief introduction to some interesting findings in mathematical cognition may put our discussion of the current topic in a better light. One of such findings is that close numbers are more difficult to compare than numbers farther apart. For example, people take longer and make more errors when they compare 2 and 3 than they compare 2 and 9. This phenomenon is commonly referred to as the *distance effect*. As mentioned earlier, fractions of unlike denominators, for their inconsistency with the value scheme of whole numbers, are more difficult to compare than fractions of like denominators. When the more difficult case of fractions (like numerators and unlike denominators) is combined with the more difficult case under the distance effect (numbers close to each other such as 5 and 6), it is small wonder that Jane's children would make frequent errors. A closer look of Figure 12.4 reveals that the shaded areas in the two pizzas are not very different.

Once Jane becomes aware of the distance effect, she can make an informed decision on what examples to use for comparing fractions of unlike denominators. For the current topic, her children's understanding can be greatly enhanced if she could make the denominators in the two fractions substantially different from each other. They could be 5 and 24, or they could be 4 and 30. If Jane does not intend to draw any figures, she could make them as different as 5 and 200. When the two pieces of pizza are substantially different from each other because the denominators used are very different (see Figure 12.5 for a comparison of $\frac{1}{5}$ and $\frac{1}{24}$), children may find them much easier to compare than the two pieces of pizza represented by fractions having denominators as close to each other as 5 and 6.

Figure 12.5 A Comparison of 1/5 (a) and 1/24 (b) Is Much Easier Because the Areas They Represent Are Very Different

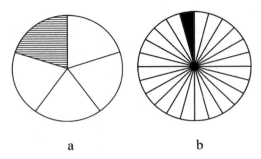

a   b

Percentage Shouldn't Be Juxtaposed with Fractions and Decimals

On the first day of teaching percentage, Jane said to her children, "We have learned fractions and decimals. Now we'll learn another form of number. It is called percentage."

In order to see the problem with what Jane said, let's explore why we need *percent* in the first place. Suppose you were a store manager and wanted to keep track of the daily performance of the 20 employees in your store. Because of the different price ranges of the merchandise sold at each department, each employee had a different goal depending on the department that employee was in. Also, sales differed from day to day, with Sunday being the busiest day and Wednesday being the slowest day of the week. Each employee had a different sales goal set for the different days of the week. For a particular day, let's suppose salesperson A in the furniture department had a goal of $1550, salesperson B in the cosmetics department had a goal of $1245, and salesperson C in the school supplies department had a goal of $815.

Now let's suppose you wanted to see, halfway through the day on a certain day, how each employee's performance in sales was. With salesperson A reaching $745, salesperson B reaching $647, and salesperson C reaching $498, how did each salesperson's sales compare to those of the others? To find out, you would need to express the sales each salesperson had reached in relation to his or her goal of the day: $\frac{745}{1550}$, $\frac{647}{1245}$, and $\frac{498}{815}$ for salespersons A, B, and C, respectively. To compare these three fractions, you would need to find the least common denominator, which is not an easy task even with the help of a small calculator when the numbers are 3- or 4-digit (the least common denominator in this example, by the way, is large: 62,909,850). The trouble is, if you wanted to compare some other employees, you would have a different set of denominators to work with because their goals were all different. Even with the same employees, as their goals were different from day to day, the denominators would also differ from day to day. Imagine the headache you would be faced with each time you needed to compare any number of sales. You would soon realize that there really should be an easier and more efficient way to do this.

This is where percentage comes into play. In order to make easy comparisons of fractions with all different denominators, mathematicians have figured out a way whereby all those fractions to be compared are changed into ones with a common denominator, 100. With this common denominator, there is no need to find the least common denominator any longer. Whatever the original denominator is, we simply change that into 100 and then change the numerator accordingly to maintain the same ratio. After this change, we can compare any number of fractions without having to go through the trouble of finding the common denominator. For the sales example, the performance of salespersons A, B, and C halfway through the day is $\frac{48}{100}$, $\frac{52}{100}$, and $\frac{61}{100}$, respectively, with the numerator rounded to the nearest whole number. Now these numbers can be easily compared. We can see that despite the largest dollar amount, salesperson A's performance actually was the lowest among the three salespersons. In contrast, the dollar amount of $498 for salesperson C, even though the lowest, translates into the highest performance.

To make it easier for reading and writing, mathematicians have devised a special symbol for expressing a fraction with a denominator of 100. The fraction bar and denominator of 100 have been transformed into the percentage sign: %. Thus, $\frac{61}{100}$ is commonly written as 61%. Conversely, when children see a percent such as 48%, they need to comprehend it as meaning $\frac{48}{100}$. (Incidentally, this concept is still expressed in two words in French: *pour cent*, meaning literally "for [every] hundred." Earlier, English had a similar form: *per cent*, but the two words have been fused together in American English.)

In summary, a percent is no different from a fraction. It is simply a fraction with a denominator of 100, for easy comparison. With this in mind, when you start teaching percentage, you may want to put it in the picture of fractions in general and say something along the line of, "We are going to learn a special fraction today. This fraction has a fixed denominator of 100."

13

Decimals

Changing the Value Scheme of Base-10 Blocks Is Not a Good Idea

Base-10 blocks are a popular manipulative set in teaching place value and, in particular, in demonstrating regrouping between columns of multidigit numbers. The unit cube represents 1. Ten such blocks, as if fused together, form a rod, which naturally represents 10. Ten such rods are fused together to form a flat, which represents 100. Finally, 10 flats are fused together and form a thousand cube, which, just as its name indicates, represents 1000.

Jane used those blocks extensively while teaching addition and subtraction involving regrouping such as 35 − 18 and many other topics, and they worked very well. Now that it was time for her children to learn decimal numbers, she thought of those blocks again and wanted to take advantage of them in this new task. This is what she said to her children one day: "We used those blocks before. But in order to deal with our decimal numbers now, we need to change what each block represents. The flat doesn't represent 100 anymore. Now it represents 1 for us. If we break this flat into 10 equal parts, then one such part is a rod, which we write as 0.1. If we further divide this rod into 10 equal parts, then each such part is this smallest block, which we write as 0.01."

This is exactly where the problem lies. Ever since her children were exposed to base-10 blocks, they learned that a unit block is 1, a rod is 10, and a flat is 100. This value scheme may very well have taken root in them. Now suddenly Jane wanted to change it: She wanted these same blocks to represent a different set of values. Naturally, some of her children got confused.

Changing the value scheme of base-10 blocks for the discussion of decimal numbers is not a good idea. First of all, every block can potentially represent two different values. For example, does a set of 2 rods and 3 unit blocks represent 23 or 0.23? Here Jane may find herself having to give the two schemes two different labels such as "whole number blocks" versus "decimal number blocks." But a more serious problem occurs when both schemes need to be used to represent a number such as 101.25. By Jane's new value scheme 1.25 is represented by 1 flat, 2 rods, and 5 unit blocks. But how would she represent the 1 in the hundreds place of 101.25? Using another flat? How would her children be able to tell which flat is 100 and which flat is 1? Or would they use 101 flats? That's not very constructive.

By now, a question may surface: "If changing the value scheme of base-10 blocks is not a good idea, then what can I use to teach decimal numbers?"

Two things may be good candidates. One is money, limited to bills of multiples of 10 such as $100, $10, $1, and coins of dimes and pennies. Since the way an amount is written (such as 1.25 and 0.75) is consistent with the actual value scheme (one $1 bill = 10 dimes, one dime = 10 pennies) and also since prices in decimal form are everywhere, from grocery stores to television commercials, these money bills and coins make a good manipulative set for teaching decimal numbers. But a drawback for money units is their lack of physical connection between different units. For example, a $10 bill is not physically 10 times larger or longer than a $1 bill, and a dime is even smaller in size than a penny.

The other is the meter tape measure. A meter is divided into 10 decimeters, and a decimeter is divided into 10 centimeters. A meter, a decimeter, and a centimeter are represented by 1, 0.1, and 0.01 (m), respectively, and these are exactly how they are written in real life. A good thing about the meter tape measure is it doesn't have the drawback that money has. Since the tape measure's intended use is for measuring length, the relation between different units is in their actual lengths: 1 meter is physically 10 times a decimeter, and 1 decimeter is physically 10 times a centimeter. Also, a meter tape measure is inexpensive and may be cut into pieces for teaching purposes.

When Is It Appropriate to Read a Decimal as a Fraction?

In teaching her children about how to read a decimal, Jane tried to make a connection to their prior knowledge of fractions. This is what she said: "In reading a decimal number, first you need to separate your number into two parts: the whole number part, which is before the decimal point, and the decimal part, the part after the decimal point. You already know how to read a whole number. Then treat the part after the decimal point just as a fraction. Connect the two parts with the word *and*. For example, read 3.25 as 'three and twenty-five hundredths.'"

It's true that most decimals can be transformed into fractions, and reading a decimal as a fraction can enable children to see the interconnectedness between them. But we have to recognize that reading a decimal as a fraction has serious limitations and flaws, and, in certain circumstances, it's next to impossible to do so. Let's look into such limitations and flaws.

The first problem is that when the number of decimal digits increases, reading a decimal as a fraction becomes anywhere between clumsy and impossible. Handling quite a few decimal digits is not too distant a prospect for current elementary children, as they will soon go into middle and high schools, and many into universities, where that scenario is not unusual. Let's use the value of π as an example. π is a never-ending decimal number. At two or three digits, it doesn't seem to be a problem, as 3.14 can be read as "three and fourteen hundredths" and 3.142 as "three and one hundred forty-two thousandths." But what about $\pi \approx 3.1415927$? Or $\pi \approx 3.1415926536$? Or $\pi \approx 3.141592653589793$? A more important question is: Even if you could read it as a fraction, will other people understand you? You may do a simple experiment. Compose a number of 10 decimal digits such as 8.2793415086 (not to mention anything longer) and ask the teacher next door to read it as a fraction. Write down what that teacher has said and ask another teacher to translate it back into an Arabic number. Can you guarantee that you will get the original number back?

Then there is the problem of using the word *and*. At least for some people, it is customary to say *and* in reading a 3-digit number in English, as in "one hundred and twenty-three" for 123. Now when a decimal is read as a fraction, the decimal point is "translated" as *and*. This creates a problem when there are two *and*s in a number, which can be very difficult to interpret, as in "four hundred and three thousand two hundred and sixty-five ten-thousandths" (is it 403,200.0065 or 400.3265?). To avoid this scenario, some teachers forbid their children to say *and* in expressing 3-digit numbers. But this doesn't mean that adults will stop saying it, which, potentially, would result in confusion if two *and*s happen to be used within one number.

Taken as a whole, reading a decimal as a fraction is essentially a roundabout process where the speaker first translates the decimal into a fraction and then the listener translates the fraction back into a decimal. This translation process has two direct consequences. First, it takes much longer than reading a decimal just as a decimal. Second, it's prone to error. If you do the abovementioned experiment on several people, don't be surprised that the answers you get are all different.

But most importantly, decimals are *not* read as fractions in daily life. The following Math in Action box lists a few actual instances of how decimals are read by newscasters, sports commentators, and other programs on television. If you collect all instances of how decimals are read on television for a specified period of time, you will find that those read as fractions are few and far between.

☑ **Math in Action: Instances of how Decimals Are Read (in Italics) on Television between March and May, 2016**

- News reporter, on CNN: "But last year, his attorneys argued that the course was worth far less, only *one point three five* million dollars."
- Narrator of *Forensic Files*, on HLN: "Hair grows at an average rate of *one point three* centimeters per month."
- Commentator on a men's basketball game, on ESPN: "*Three point five* seconds remain for being uneliminated. . ."
- Commercial on TENNIS: "You'll simply earn unlimited *one point five* percent cash back on every purchase everywhere."
- Movie, on HBO: "I do have a GPS and a *four point O* GPA."

In short, reading decimals just as decimals (namely, reading 3.14159 as "three point one four one five nine") is straightforward, fast, doesn't allow much room for misinterpretation, and can handle any number of digits beyond the decimal point. Above all, that is the way people read them in daily lives.

You may ask, "When is it appropriate to read a decimal as a fraction?"

There are indeed times when it's appropriate to read a decimal as a fraction. Two conditions usually need to be present for it to occur. First, there's no whole number part, and that eliminates the necessity of using *and* to represent a decimal point. Second, there's only one significant decimal digit, so that the formulation is simple. This one significant digit often falls on a "neat" column or strongly suggests a certain column. For example, *0.000001 second* can be read as "one millionth of a second" rather than "zero point zero zero zero zero zero one second." The following Math in Action box shows an example from coverage of an NCAA gymnastics championship competition on television. Keep in mind, though, this way of treating a decimal is more "interpreting" than directly "reading."

☑ **Math in Action: An NCAA Gymnastics Championship Competition**

After three rotations, these scores were shown on the television screen:

- University A: 98.8500
- University B: 98.6125
- University C: 98.6000

The commentator said, "University A [is first], with an outstanding ninety-eight eight five, University B is second, about *two tenths* of a point behind."

25.0 and 25 Aren't Exactly the Same

In calculating decimal numbers, Jane's children often ended up with one or more trailing 0s after the decimal point such as 25.0. In a situation like this, Jane would tell them to simply leave off the trailing 0s. For this example, she told them, "25.0 and 25 are exactly the same. So simply omit the 0 and write 25."

This actually depends on what is being described. Let's take a closer look at that.

On the one hand, the amount or quantity being described may be discrete. In this case, there are no intermediate values between any member and its next neighbor. For example, suppose you have 25 children in your class. Each child is discrete, and there are no intermediate values between any two of them. If you are sending them out to the water fountain in groups, you may line them up and say, "The first five children go. The rest of us stay here and wait." You will not say, "The first 5.3 children go." There is no value between the fifth and sixth children.

On the other hand, the amount or quantity being described may be continuous. There may be an infinite number of intermediate values between any two points on the scale. Suppose you put water in a test tube and heat it from 25°C to 26°C. An infinite number of values can be used to describe the temperatures in between: 25.1°, 25.15°, 25.384°, and so on.

Thus, if you had a thermometer with whole-degree readings and you measured your classroom temperature to be 25°C, it wasn't exactly, or exclusively, 25°. Rather, it was anywhere between 24.5° and 25.5° (to be more accurate, the range should be expressed as $24.5 \leq x < 25.5$). This range of temperatures can be illustrated in Figure 13.1, where any point on the bold line segment can be represented by 25°.

Figure 13.1 The Range of Temperatures Covered by 25°C

Figure 13.2 The Range of Temperatures Covered by 25.0°C

If your thermometer was accurate to one decimal place—that is, its markings were 23.1, 23.2, 23.3, etc., and you measured your classroom temperature to be 25.0°—this temperature would have a much smaller range. Specifically, it would be anywhere between 24.95°C and 25.05°C (more accurately expressed as $24.95 \leq x < 25.05$). Figure 13.2 illustrates this range.[1]

A comparison of Figures 13.1 and 13.2 suggests that these two numbers, 25 and 25.0, represent two different ranges of temperatures, with 25.0 being more accurate than 25. While the temperature represented by 25°C may actually include a reading of 25.4°, the temperature represented by 25.0° certainly doesn't include a reading of 25.4°. By the same token, 25.00 is even more accurate, with a yet smaller range between 24.995 and 25.005.

To sum up, trailing 0s for describing continuous quantities are *not* meaningless. They usually indicate a more accurate range.

In teaching children how to represent decimal numbers, what you want to do is specify the number of decimal places to round to and ask your children to keep that number of decimal places, even though such numbers may contain trailing 0s. For example, if the representation of the final answer of 21.7 + 3.3 calls for one decimal place and your children calculate it to be 25.0, then they need to write it that way instead of writing it as 25.

Keep a Few More Decimal Places when Rounding at Intermediate Steps

It's true that in dealing with decimal numbers we often need to round. However, it's important to realize that an inappropriate rounding at intermediate steps may cause the final answer to be way off. The direction to "round to the nearest whole number," "round to the nearest tenth," and so on is usually intended for the final answer, not intermediate steps.

Take the problem $(6 + 20 \div 7)^3$ for example. Let's say the direction says "Round to the nearest tenth." After Jane's children executed the first step,

$20 \div 7$, they found that they got a nonterminating decimal: 2.857143. So Jane directed them to round to the nearest tenth. They finished the problem in this way, shown in the following Math in Action box.

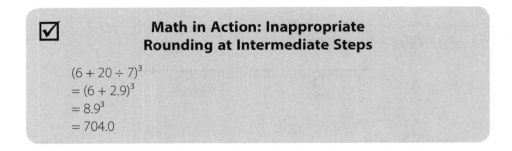

Math in Action: Inappropriate Rounding at Intermediate Steps

$(6 + 20 \div 7)^3$
$= (6 + 2.9)^3$
$= 8.9^3$
$= 704.0$

Let's see what happens if we keep just two more decimal places after the first step, as shown in the following Math in Action box.

Math in Action: Delay Rounding to the Desired Decimal Place until the End of the Problem

$(6 + 20 \div 7)^3$
$= (6 + 2.857)^3$
$= 8.857^3$
$= 694.8$

A difference of two decimal places when rounding at intermediate steps causes the two answers to this problem to be different by almost 10. Of course it's the answer in the previous Math in Action box (704.0) that's more off. If the exponent was higher, the error could be even greater. If this was for solving a real-world problem, such an error could bring about serious consequences.

Jane's directions could be modified just a little to avoid misinterpretations on her children's part. Instead of a general requirement of "Round to the nearest whole number," "Round to the nearest tenth," and so on, you may want to try this: "Round your final answer to the nearest whole number," "Round your final answer to the nearest tenth," and so on. For intermediate results, if your children are using calculators, have them use whatever number of decimal places displayed. If somehow they have to round and reenter an intermediate value, then have them keep two or three more decimal places, at a minimum, than what is required of the final answer.

Note

1 Conventionally, the left endpoint of this range should be a solid circle, meaning this point (24.95) is part of the range, whereas the right endpoint should be a hollow circle, meaning this point (25.05) is not part of the range. This detail has to be left out in this figure as the range covered is so small.

14

Simple Statistics and Graphs

Were the Children in Your Class Born, on Average, on the 12.8th?

On the day Jane was teaching simple statistics, she asked each child to write down the day of the month on which he or she was born (1–31). After she collected the raw data, she involved her children in calculating the mean, median, and mode of the set of numbers on a calculator. All went well, and after they punched in the numbers and hit the Enter key, her children came up with the three measures.

But here's the problem: How would Jane explain or interpret the results of the calculations? Suppose the mean, median, and mode for the dataset were 12.8, 14.5 and 18, respectively. What did these numbers mean? Could she possibly say, "The children in our class, on average, were born on the 12.8th?" So the point to make here is, when raw data are collected from real-world situations, they should be able to answer questions concerning such situations. Otherwise the results may be meaningless.

The confusion over Jane's class activity arose because the data she collected weren't strictly quantitative. For brevity purposes, we can divide data into two major types: qualitative and quantitative. Many qualitative data are nominal in nature and have verbal descriptors as their original form, such as black, brown, and blue for eye color, and Catholic, Protestant, and Jewish for religion. The nominal nature in such data is easy to ascertain, as people won't try to find the "mean eye color" or the "median religion."

Quantitative data, on the other hand, are numerical. Such data express either a countable quantity such as the number of siblings a child has (discrete), or a measurement of some physical dimension such as a child's height in centimeters (continuous).

The data Jane collected, the day of the month each child was born on, had a disguise—their values were numerical and may appear to be quantitative. However, they weren't true quantitative data. If Jane had collected the year, the month, and the day on which each of her children was born and converted those numbers into age in number of days, then those would be true quantitative data. For example, a child whose age was 3425 days would be 10 days older than a child who was 3415 days old, and Jane may say that the youngest child in her class was 3208 days old, and so on. However, when her children reported the days of the month they were born on, no similar descriptions were possible. A child who was born on the 24th may not necessarily be younger than a child who was born on the 20th because their birth months and even birth years could be different. Similarly, a child who was born on the 1st may not be the oldest, as any child born in the previous month (e.g., May 31 vs. June 1) in the same year was older.

To tell whether the data collected are quantitative so that you can perform some simple statistics on, you can do two simple tests by asking: (a) Can the data be ordered such that the ranking is consistent with the actual ranking? (b) Is it appropriate to compare the distance between values? The data Jane collected on the day of the month fail both of these two tests (all her children, when ordered from the 1st, 2nd, and so on till the 31st, aren't necessarily from the oldest to the youngest, and it's not the case that a child born on the 10th was older than a child born on the 20th). Thus, the days her children were born on were merely used as labels, and they were by and large nominal data just as eye color or religion.

To enable your children to come up with data in connection with their daily lives in order to compute the mean, median, and mode, you may want to use such quantitative data as their heights in centimeters; the number of books each child has read during the past 6 months; or age in years, months, or even days. Then after their calculations, you may sum up the results by saying that the mean height of the children in your class is how many centimeters, or each child in your class, on average, has read this number of books during the past 6 months, or the median age of your children was this number of years, months, or days.

"The Mean Is the Average"

In teaching simple statistics, Jane picked up the first three most common measures covered in textbooks for elementary students: the mean, median, and mode. This is how she taught these concepts and the ways to find them: "For a dataset, the mean is the average. Add up all the values and then divide the sum by the number of items. The median is the middle number. First arrange all the numbers in either ascending or descending order and pick the one that lies in the middle. If there are an even number of items, pick the two at the middle, add them up, and divide the result by 2. The mode is the value that occurs the most frequently."

Although what Jane said about the mean being the average is not conceptually wrong, the way she presented the three indices—that is, discussing all three measures at the same time but reserving the word *average* for only the mean—left her children with the impression that only the mean is the average while the median and the mode are not. To discuss this topic in more detail, let's first look at what these three measures are used for.

It's very often the case that after we collect a set of data, we don't want to present all individual scores to other people. Let's consider two scenarios. For the first scenario, suppose you recently gave your class of 24 children a math test. When you mentioned this to the principal, she asked, "How did your kids do?" It's unlikely that you would read out all 24 individual scores to her. This is where a measure for the *central tendency* becomes useful. You would more than likely give her a most representative score. For the second scenario, suppose you plan to run a babysitting business and you're deciding between two parts of town for the location of your business. The key factor to consider is the number of 3- through 5-year-old children each family within the two parts of town has. You send off a survey team to obtain these numbers. Several days later, the survey team comes back with the number of children from 1600 families in one part of town and that from 1450 families in the other. It probably won't help you very much if these numbers are reported to you individually, such as 3, 1, 2, 4, 0, 2, 1. . . Instead, you may want your survey team to summarize the data and report to you one representative figure from each part of town. In both scenarios, the *representative figure*, as the name indicates, best captures where all individual data points stand and best represents the whole dataset, but in a simplified way. This representative figure is commonly known as the average. It describes the central tendency.

Several indices can be used to describe the central tendency depending on what type of data is being described and some other factors. Most often the mean is used. But sometimes the mean isn't the best index for certain types of data and, in particular, doesn't handle outliers well. For example, in describing the average household income for a particular city, the mean can be easily distorted when there are a few households that earn so much that they can drive up the mean to such a degree that it's no longer representative. That's why the median is often used in reporting average household income. By this measure, the outliers, namely, the extreme scores, no longer affect the central tendency. But the key point is, the mean, median, and mode are all ways to describe the average.

In short, when you teach the central tendency, you can either mention that the mean, median, and mode are all indices for reporting the average—or you can avoid using the word *average* altogether. That way you will not be creating a misconception that the mean is the average while the median and mode are not.

Where in the World Does the Mode Ever Get Used?

Jane was very familiar with the textbook definition of the mean, median, and mode. While teaching this topic, she sometimes came up with her own datasets and had her children practice finding the three indices. For example, the following Math in Action box shows two datasets Jane assigned one day, followed by the mean, median, and mode that her children calculated.

Math in Action: Two Sets of Data Jane Assigned for Finding the Mean, Median, and Mode

Set A: 2, 3, 4, 5, 6, 8, 8.
Mean = 5.1, median = 5, mode = 8.

Set B: 2, 2, 6, 7, 8, 9, 11, 12.
Mean = 7.1, median = 7.5, mode = 2.

Technically, there was nothing wrong with these calculations. However, while the mean and median derived from these datasets captured the central tendency quite well, the mode gave a rather distorted picture. As discussed earlier, all the three indices—the mean, median, and mode—are measures of the central tendency of a dataset, and each one of them is used to answer the question: "What's the average of this dataset?" or "What's the most representative number for this dataset?" However, the mode in both datasets, 8 and 2 respectively, was far from the central point of the dataset. In fact, lying at either the lowest or highest end of the datasets, they didn't even come close to representing the central tendency at all. Suppose dataset A was the record of the number of children each of the seven employees in an office had. Would anyone ever say that the average number of children these seven people had was 8? In other words, people normally would not use the mode as the measure for representing the central tendency of this dataset.

You may ask, "I see the mean used in daily life all the time. And I occasionally see the median used, such as the median household income in census reports. But where in the world does the mode ever get used, if at all?"

There are situations where it makes good sense to use the mode as a representative number of a dataset. Let's suppose you taught two classes during the past two years, one a first-grade class and the other a third-grade class. Let's further suppose that there were 25 children in each of the two classes. The following Math in Action box shows the frequency distribution of the children's ages in these two classes.

☑ **Math in Action: Frequency Distribution of Students' Age, in Years, in Jane's Two Classes**

First-Grade Class	
Age	**Number of Children**
5	2
6	20
7	3
Third-Grade Class	
Age	**Number of Children**
6	1
7	3
8	21

With regard to your first-grade class, if someone asks you about the average age of the children, the mode is the easiest, most readily accessible index to use: 6. Because the overwhelming majority of your children (20 of them) were of this age, the mode wouldn't be far away from the mean age anyway. In other words, the mode captures the central tendency very well in this situation. If you use a calculator and actually calculate the mean, you will find that the two indices are almost identical: 6 versus 6.04.

Even though the mode may be at the end of an ordered dataset as in the case of your third-grade class, where the mode is 8 (the oldest age in this group), still, using this index as its average won't be far off. A calculation reveals that the mean of this dataset is 7.8, which is very close to 8, the mode. The reason for the mode's being at the end of the ordered dataset but still being close to the mean is that its frequency is substantially higher than the other data points combined (21 vs. 4). In a sense, it "overpowers" the other data points and essentially dominates the whole set to be the representative figure. In contrast, almost all the seven data points in dataset A described at the beginning of this section were unique, except for the two cases of 8. This mere one more case does not make the data point of 8 more representative than any other one. If it's singled out as an average of the whole dataset simply because it has one more case than all other data points, it can tremendously distort the whole picture and can be very misleading. That's why nobody would feel comfortable concluding that "the average number of children the seven people in this office had was 8."

In summary, a condition for using the mode as a measure of central tendency is that its frequency is *substantially* higher than any other data point such that it won't give a distorted picture.

Do All Your Children Have an Equal Chance of Winning?

In teaching math concepts to elementary children, Jane tried at every chance possible to relate to their daily life or even to the children themselves. But sometimes this doesn't work out very well. The following Math in Action box shows a problem Jane gave one day when she was teaching probability.

> ☑ **Math in Action: Jane's Problem on Probability**
>
> Ms. Smith is having her class run a 100-meter race. There are 12 girls and 8 boys in her class. What's the probability of a girl winning the race?

And here's how Jane led her class in figuring out the probability:

$$p = \frac{number\,of\,girls}{total\,number\,of\,children} = \frac{12}{20} = 0.6$$

An important condition for this formula is that all events have an equal chance of occurring. That is, this formula will work if there's no gender difference in running a race and every child, as compared to any other child, has an equal chance of winning. In real life, however, we know that boys and girls perform differently. That difference can affect the prediction of the outcome of the race. In other words, not fulfilling this "equal chance" condition can lead to a faulty probability.

To make an analogy, suppose 99 children and 1 adult were to run a race. You probably wouldn't say that a child winning this race was 99%. Just on the contrary, even though the one adult was outnumbered considerably, that single person still had a much better chance of winning. Similarly, if you bet on a race between a man and a woman, you most likely would bet on the man winning the race, all other conditions being equal.

For the purpose of modifying the problem mentioned earlier, you have to ensure the satisfaction of the condition of equal chance for everybody or every event. If you take a close look at the revised version of the problem shown in the following Math in Action box, you will find that this condition has been met and can be used for calculating the probability.

☑ **Math in Action: A Revised Version
of the Previous Problem**

Ms. Smith has prepared a deck of cards and written every child's name on a card. There are 12 girls and 8 boys in her class. If Ms. Smith shuffles the cards and draws one without looking, what's the probability of her drawing a girl's name?

Use Different Types of Data for a Beginning Lesson on Graphs

On the first day of teaching graphs, Jane announced that it was "Pockets Day" that day and started off collecting data on the number of pockets on her children's clothes. She first figured out that the largest number of pockets on any child's clothes would be no more than 6. Then she drew a horizontal line (the *x*-axis) representing the number of pockets a child might have. Next she asked each child to count the number of pockets on his or her own clothes and write that number down on a sticky note she had just given out. She then counted the number of times each number of pockets had shown up on the sticky notes and drew a corresponding bar above the horizontal line. Her graph now looked like this (see Figure 14.1).

Here's a problem with a graph like this at the beginning stage: The two groups of numbers were interfering with each other. This can be revealed by a look at the questions Jane had to ask. After graphing the data collected, Jane asked a series of questions such as "What's the number of pockets that most children have?," "What's the number of pockets that the fewest children have?," "How many children have 3 pockets?," and "What's the smallest number of pockets that children have?" Even though Jane marked the *x*-axis and *y*-axis as representing "Number of Pockets" and "Number of Children," respectively, because they both represented quantitative data and the numbers used were in a similar range, her children could easily be confused about which was which. Take the first question "What's the number of pockets that most children have?" for example. Some children may look at the bar at the far end of the *x*-axis and find 6 there. Still other children may locate the tallest bar and call out its frequency, 6, on the *y*-axis. In a similar fashion, statements

Figure 14.1 Number of Children by the Number of Pockets They Had

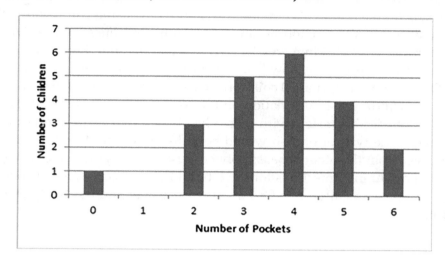

Figure 14.2 Number of Children by the Color of Shirts They Were Wearing

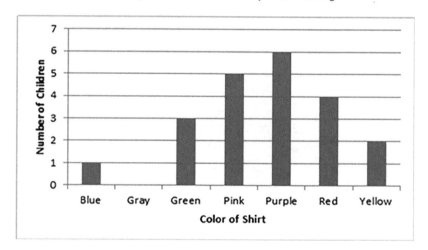

such as "1 child has 0 pockets and 0 children have one pocket" can be difficult to comprehend.

A way to avoid this situation is to use qualitative data for the x-axis while keeping the quantitative data on the y-axis. For example, instead of polling on the number of pockets (quantitative data) her children have, Jane may want to poll on different colors (qualitative data) of the shirts they are wearing. Or she may want to poll on the different types of pizza (qualitative data) her children prefer. A similar set of data collected on the different colors of the shirts they're wearing may be represented by the graph displayed in Figure 14.2.

Now, even if we ask similar questions to those asked about the number of pockets on the children's clothes, the chance of causing confusion will be greatly reduced. When children are faced with such questions as "What's the color that most children wear?", "What's the total number of colors that children are wearing?", "How many children are wearing green shirts?", and "What color of shirt are 0 children wearing?", children will have a much easier time finding the information on the correct axis. In a sense, these two types of data don't interfere with each other. Whatever the question is, when it concerns one type of data, it would be unlikely for children to search for the answer from the other type, simply because answers from one type (3, 4, or 5) will not fit into questions for the other (blue, red, or yellow). Therefore, it will be easier for children to find the correct answer and less likely to make mistakes.

15

Measurement

Why Do We Need Nonstandard Measurement?

It was time to take up the topic on nonstandard measurement, and Jane started off with telling her children the rationale for it. She said, "Sometimes we want to measure the length of something, but realize we don't have the necessary tools handy such as a ruler or a tape measure. In such a situation, we use what we can find at the time such as straws, pencils, or even our arms or hands as measuring tools. Today we'll use pencils to measure how long our desks are."

It's true that people sometimes do use concrete objects as makeshift tools for measuring other objects. But the rationale for teaching nonstandard measurement in an elementary school classroom is not for addressing the unavailability of measuring tools. Even though there may be a ruler or even a tape measure in a child's box of supplies, we still want to start off teaching nonstandard measurement. The rationale for doing this, then, is for developing children's initial understanding of the basic principles underlying measurement and laying the foundation for their applying these principles when they encounter standard measurement in later grades.

With this in mind, instruction on nonstandard measurement should align with the essential elements involved in using standard measuring tools. The following Math in Action box lists the three essential elements when measuring the length of an object, such as a desktop, using a standard measuring tool. Adults often take for granted the conditions that must be satisfied in order to make an accurate measurement, but these conditions have to be specifically taught to children.

> ☑ **Math in Action: Essential Elements for an Accurate Measurement of Length Using a Tape Measure**
>
> - Point 0 on the tape measure is lined up with one of the endpoints of the object.
> - The tape measure is pulled straight.
> - The point on the tape measure that corresponds to other endpoint of the object is located. Reading of this point on the tape measure is taken as the length of the object.

Corresponding to the essential elements for measuring the length of an object using a tape measure, the activity Jane described at the beginning of her class about using pencils to measure the length of a desktop should contain these elements, as presented in the following Math in Action box.

> ☑ **Math in Action: Essential Elements for Measuring the Length of a Desktop Using Pencils**
>
> - The endpoint of the first pencil (point 0) is lined up with the edge of the desk (one of its endpoints).
> - All additional pencils are lined up straight, end to end, with no gaps or overlaps in between.
> - The total number of pencils covering the desktop from one end to the other is taken as the length of the desktop.

You will notice that the accurateness of measurement using nonstandard measuring tools leaves much to be desired. But for children at this stage, accurateness is less of a concern than learning the essential elements involved in taking such measurement. That's the purpose for using nonstandard measurement.

What Is Standard Measurement?

When it came to using a ruler to measure the length of an object, Jane wanted to base that discussion on the experience her children already had. So she said, "We already know some common units for measuring length in our daily lives such as yards, feet, and inches. These are standard units. We are going to learn metric units today. The first three units for measuring length we are going to learn today are meters, centimeters, and millimeters."

It is interesting to note that some people use the term *standard measurement* in nonstandard ways. Colloquially, *standard* is often used to refer to something that came into being earlier or something that has been used for a longer period of time. This is the case with describing shifting gears of a vehicle. Some people refer to manual shift as standard, in juxtaposition with automatic shift. Since this way of using *standard* does not cause any significant confusion, we don't have to be concerned.

When it comes to describing systems of measurement, however, this use of the word *standard* does cause confusion. Currently two systems of measurement are in use world wide: the metric system (which employs *meter, kilogram,* and *liter* for the three most common attributes of length, weight, and volume) and the customary system (which employs *foot, pound,* and *gallon* for those three attributes). Some people use *standard* to refer to the customary system, leaving on children the impression that the metric system is nonstandard.

In fact, both the customary system and metric system are standard, and both can be very accurate. The difference lies in the fact that the metric system is strictly base-10 and employs much fewer names. It's currently used in most countries all over the world. The customary system, in contrast, uses many different bases and employs many names and conversion ratios. Only three countries in the world still use it: Liberia, Myanmar, and the United States. Nonstandard measurement, as we discussed earlier, refers to the use of common objects such as pencils, paper clips, and even body parts such as hands and arms, in measuring some other objects. We usually teach children nonstandard measurement before we teach them standard measurement.

The relationship among these different systems of measurement can be illustrated in Figure 15.1.

Figure 15.1 Relationship Among Different Systems of Measurement

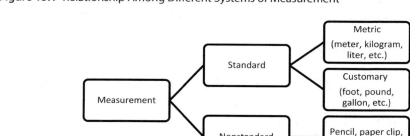

What Are Centimeters Used to Measure?

After teaching her children nonstandard measurement such as measuring the length of their desks with pencils, the width of a storybook with paper clips, and the height of a poster with their hands, Jane decided to introduce standard measurement units. In particular, she wanted to start teaching metric units first. So she said, "Today, we'll learn how to use centimeters to measure length, width, and height, and then we'll use grams to measure weight."

Unlike *weight*, which is the only word used to describe the attribute of how heavy an object is (in most cases, *weight* and *mass* are exchangeable, but they aren't exactly the same thing in physics), there're several terms to describe the attribute of how long an object is: *length*, *width*, and *height* (these are the three most common ones. There're others such as *depth* and *thickness*). These three terms, however, don't describe three different attributes. Instead, they all describe the same attribute: the distance from one end of an object to its other end along one dimension. When this attribute is described in its general sense, one term is sufficient: *length*. Just as weight is used to refer to how heavy an object is, length can be similarly used to refer to the general attribute of how long something is.

Thus, we need to distinguish the general sense of the word *length* and its narrow sense. On one hand, when we talk about the attribute of distance, *length* is the general term to use and it includes width, height, and so on. On the other hand, when we talk about different dimensions within this attribute, we use *length*, *width*, and *height* for this purpose, and *length* here is used in its narrow sense. Thus, back to what Jane told her children concerning what centimeters are used to measure, she was using the general sense of distance, and in that case, the word *length* alone is sufficient.

You might argue, if *length*, *width*, and *height* all describe the same attribute, why do we need to have three terms instead of just one? To answer this question, let's look at one specific example. Suppose we have a rectangular prism with dimensions of 3 cm × 2 cm × 5 cm (see Figure 15.2) and need to know its volume. To find out, we use the formula $v = l \cdot w \cdot h$, where l, w, and h stand for *length*, *width*, and *height*, respectively. For the problem at hand, the volume is

$$v = l \cdot w \cdot h = 3 \cdot 2 \cdot 5 = 30 \text{ cm}^3.$$

Here, in order to find the volume of the rectangular prism, we need to know its three dimensions—that is, its length, width, and height—and they can all be different. If there was only one term to use, then the formula $v = l \cdot l \cdot l$ can be used only if all the three dimensions are the same. Apparently this is not sufficient, for there are rectangular prisms made of three different

Figure 15.2 A Rectangular Prism of Dimensions 3 cm × 2 cm × 5 cm

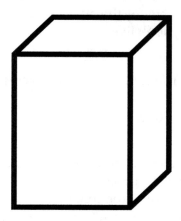

dimensions, and we do need to be able to describe these different dimensions. It's here that we have different terms for such a task.

Leave Out Units of Measure at Intermediate Steps

In teaching how to calculate the area of an equilateral rectangle given the length of one side, Jane said, "Suppose the side is 3 centimeters. Square this number, and you'll get the area of this equilateral rectangle." She first wrote the formula $A = s^2$ on the board, and then replaced s with 3 cm. Now the expression became $A = s^2 = 3$ cm ^{2}. Finally, she calculated the result to be 9 cm². The whole expression on the board now was: $A = s^2 = 3$ cm $^2 = 9$ cm².

Here is a problem: What Jane showed to her children is not an equality. That is, if she omitted the cm^2 part, what she had on the left side of the last equal sign doesn't equal what she had on its right side (3 = 9 certainly doesn't make sense). Moreover, if the same logic Jane applied to 3 cm² = 9 cm² was reapplied to the result, then she would get an expression that could go on forever, without reaching any result: 3 cm² = 9 cm² = 81 cm² = 6561 cm²...

Jane might protest, "I left some space after 3 centimeters before I wrote the exponent." Here a little space won't change the way a mathematical expression is evaluated, and it won't accomplish what she had intended to accomplish.

To properly handle demonstrating the procedure for solving this problem, Jane would need to do one of two things. First, enclosing 3 cm in parentheses will effectively avoid the 3 = 9 mistake. So what she should be presenting will look like $A = (3$ cm$)^2 = 9$ cm². But sometimes if a unit of measure is repeatedly used in an expression, it can look clumsy. For example, if a trapezoid has 5 cm for one of its bases, 9 cm for the other, and 10 cm for its height, then the calculation of its area may look like:

$$A = \frac{1}{2} \cdot (base_1 + base_2) \cdot height = \frac{1}{2} \cdot (5\,\text{cm} + 9\,\text{cm}) \cdot 10\,\text{cm}$$
$$= \frac{1}{2} \cdot 14\,\text{cm} \cdot 10\,\text{cm} = 70\,\text{cm}^2$$

All those units of measure scattered within the expression can potentially be distractive in the calculation process—and this isn't a complicated formula. A simpler way of handling this situation, then, is to omit the units of measure at the intermediate steps and then use whatever the unit is at the very last step. So the problem can be solved in a cleaner and more concise way:

$$A = \frac{1}{2} \cdot (base_1 + base_2) \cdot height = \frac{1}{2} \cdot (5 + 9) \cdot 10 = \frac{1}{2} \cdot 14 \cdot 10 = 70\,(\text{cm}^2)$$

How Do You Say the Word for "1000 Meters"?

As her children already had some home experience with common measures of the customary system, that is, *foot, pound, and gallon,* Jane planned a comprehensive unit on the metric system. She started with the basic units for length, weight, and volume—*meter, gram,* and *liter*—and said that one of the nicest things about the metric system is that there're much fewer names and conversion ratios to memorize than there are for the customary system. The customary system has a different set of names for each attribute. For length, it's *mile, yard, foot, inch,* and so on; for weight, it's *pound, ounce, dram,* and so on; and for volume, it's *gallon, quart, pint, cup,* and so on. In contrast, the metric system uses some prefixes across all the common measures: *kilo-* (1000), *centi-* (1/100), and *milli-* (1/1000) attached to the basic unit of *meter, gram,* and *liter.* For example, 1000 meters is a *kilometer,* 1000 grams is a *kilogram,* and 1000 liters is a *kiloliter.* After this explanation, Jane led her children in reading these words aloud. She pronounced the first word, *kilometer,* as /ki-'lo-me-ter/, in a similar way as *odometer* is pronounced.

Although *kilometer* may be pronounced either as /ki-'lo-me-ter/ or as /'ki-lo-me-ter/ and that both pronunciations are acceptable in dictionaries, pronouncing it with the second syllable stressed is not very helpful to children. To see the problem with it, let's do a little research on some words containing *meter.*

Meter is the basic unit measure for length in the metric system. As mentioned, it's combined with prefixes such as *kilo-, centi-,* and *milli-* to form larger or smaller units than the basic one, such as *kilometer, centimeter,* and *millimeter.* Let's call these words "length words" as they all measure length. They are usually pronounced with the first syllable stressed, as in /ˈcen-ti-me-ter/ and /ˈmi-lli-me-ter/.

Meanwhile, *meter* is also used to form the names of instruments used for measuring a certain attribute, such as *odometer* ([*h*]*odo-* means road in Greek) and *thermometer* (*thermo-* means heat). Let's call this group of words "instrument words." Their pronunciation, unlike that for those "length words," follows the pattern for most English words with multiple syllables, that is, the stress falls on the third syllable from the last. Thus these last two words are pronounced as /o-ˈdo-me-ter/ and /ther-ˈmo-me-ter/, respectively.

It's interesting that only *kilometer* from the group of "length words" has been singled out to be pronounced as an "instrument word," with the third syllable from the last stressed. But this pronunciation doesn't reflect the composition of the word, as the other "length words" do, and it interferes with children's learning of the prefix of *kilo-.* When pronounced this way, the two constituent parts (*kilo + meter*) seem to be fused together and give the impression that it is an "instrument word." With this pronunciation, children may not easily recognize that the word contains a *kilo* part, as *kiloliter* does.

In short, pronouncing *kilometer* as /ki-ˈlo-me-ter/ isn't helpful to children learning the metric system at the beginning stage. For this reason, it's important that we teach children to say *kilometer* as we say *kiloliter,* not as we say *odometer. Merriam-Webster's Collegiate Dictionary* (10th edition) notes that "first syllable stress (read as /ˈki-lo-me-ter/) seems to occur with a higher rate of frequency among scientists than among nonscientists."

Fractions Don't Belong with Metric Measurements

In teaching her children how to measure length in metric units, Jane displayed part of a ruler marked in centimeters, with each one further divided into 10 smaller units. These smaller units are millimeters, indicated by the small marks within each centimeter. The one in the middle is slightly longer. Figure 15.3 shows what her children saw on the screen.

Figure 15.3 A Metric Ruler in Centimeters

Figure 15.4 A Ruler in Centimeters, but Marked With Fractions

After she showed her class how to measure the length of an object in whole centimeters, Jane wanted her children to be more accurate. So she said, "The small mark in the middle of a centimeter is halfway between the beginning of a centimeter and the end of it. That's one half centimeter. Now I'm passing out some strings. Let's measure the length of each string to the nearest half centimeter." To help her children recognize these midpoints, Jane marked on her projected ruler every half centimeter in addition to the originally marked whole centimeters. Figure 15.4 shows what it looked like now.

The problem here is that Jane mixed up metric measurements with customary ones. To see the underlying reason behind this problem, let's take a look at the key difference between the customary system and the metric system. The customary system essentially uses fractions. For length, it divides an inch into two halves, and each half is further divided into two halves, with each half of the original half being one fourth. This goes on for several more times depending on how accurate people want to be. Most rulers designed for school use are in 16ths, namely, an inch divided into 16 equal parts. Some tape measures sold in home improvement stores are in 32nds, and some steel rulers are even in 64ths. With these fractions come the clumsiness and inefficiencies in making calculations. For example, if there's a rectangular piece of wood and it measures $2\frac{13}{16}$ inches by $5\frac{27}{32}$ inches, then what's its area in square inches? Without a calculator handy, it'll take an average person quite a few minutes to find the answer—first changing each number into improper fractions, then multiplying the two denominators and the two numerators to form a new fraction, and then changing this new improper fraction back to a mixed number. Sometimes if conversions are needed, the calculations may take even longer. Suppose you were not given a number like $2\frac{13}{16}$. Instead, you were given "There're 5 bottles of milk and each bottle contains 2 gallons, 3 quarts, 1 pint, and 1 cup. What's the total volume of milk in gallons?" Now imagine timing yourself in first converting each bottle's quantity before multiplying it by 5, and then changing the results back into mixed numbers.

In contrast, the metric system uses decimals. In fact, this is its very beauty: Base-10 units (*dec-* in the very word *decimal* means 10) are consistently used, which practically eliminates the necessity of dealing with fractions. For example, meter, the basic unit for length, is divided into 10 decimeters, one decimeter is divided into 10 centimeters, one centimeter is divided into 10 millimeters, and so on. In calculations involving metric measurements, there is no need to find the common denominator, changing between mixed numbers and improper fractions, and then simplifying the results to lowest terms. The measurements for the piece of wood mentioned earlier would be approximately 7.1 cm and 14.8 cm, respectively. Finding its area in square centimeters will be much faster and much easier than finding it in square inches.

Now the problem of marking all those half centimeters becomes obvious. On a metric ruler as shown in Figure 15.3, each small mark within a centimeter indicates 0.1 cm, or 1 mm. The fifth one, therefore, indicates 0.5 cm. The reason that it's a little longer than the other millimeter marks is for easier recognition. One can easily tell that the mark right before this middle mark is 0.4 cm and the one right after it is 0.6 cm without having to count. If all the millimeter marks were all the same length, it wouldn't be as easy, especially for readings in the middle range.

Second, marking each centimeter into two halves may mislead children into thinking that there're quarter-centimeter marks and eighth-centimeter marks, while actual metric rulers don't have such marks.

Most important of all, resorting to fractions in using metric units is like, to use a cliché, carrying coals to Newcastle: It makes little sense. It's time consuming, clumsy, and prone to error.

16

Computational Estimation

Is Computational Estimation an Educated Guess?

In teaching computational estimation, the first problem Jane encountered was the definition of *estimation*. She first thought about *guess*, as she had heard the coinage *guesstimate*. After all, an estimate is not expected to be the same as an exact answer. But Jane did not feel convinced that this was a good definition. A guess could be nowhere near the correct answer. If a colleague of hers were wearing a new woolen dress and asked all the people around her "Guess how much it cost?" some answers she would hear could be really wild. Jane wanted her children to do better than just "guess." So she decided on adding a modifier: an *educated* guess.

This is a much better definition in that some prior experience or knowledge is involved in making an educated guess. Suppose from Jane's prior shopping experience at a particular store, a woolen dress was more expensive than a high-end shirt, which cost about $100, but less expensive than a woolen coat, which cost about $500. With this knowledge, an educated guess for the cost of her colleague's woolen dress would be somewhere between $100 and $500. Exactly what figure Jane were to produce would also depend on other factors such as the time of year, the style of the dress, and so on. At any rate, she factored in her prior experience and this is why an educated guess is better than just a pure "guess."

However, although an educated guess can guide a person in producing a closer figure, still it's not quite what a computational estimate is and doesn't quite capture its connotations. Let's use an example to illustrate the key points of computational estimation. Suppose you gave your children a 2-digit by 2-digit multiplication problem, 54 × 32, and asked them to give you an estimate. Many elementary school children have a strong tendency to mentally go through a previously learned written procedure to get an answer. The first thing you want to stress is that they should not resort to using paper and pencil, nor should they try to mentally applying a written procedure to work on the problem.

Without going through the written procedure, an estimate may be obtained in many different ways, very often through some type of simplification. Let's trace the mind work of three fictitious children and see how each of them may get an estimate for this problem, as shown in the following Math in Action box.

☑ **Math in Action: Three Fictitious Children's Mind Work on Estimating 54 × 32**

Child A: "I rounded 54 to 50 and 32 to 30. Then I did 50 × 30 and got 1500."
Child B: "54 is about half of 100. I first multiplied 32 by 100 and got 3200. Then I halved this number to get 1600."
Child C: "32 is about one third of 100, so I just need to find one third of 54 × 100. I know one third of 54 is 18, so one third of 54 × 100 is 18 × 100, which is 1800."

All these are valid, reasonable estimates. However, if a child rounds 54 to 100 and 32 to 30 and obtains an estimate of 3000, you'll probably think it's way off mark. After all, for a problem whose exact answer is 1728, an estimate of 3000 is about 74% off. This may not be very useful.

To conclude, at the beginning stage of teaching children what computational estimation is, you may want to stress its key characteristics: (a) obtained mentally through some type of simplification rather than through applying its written procedure, and (b) the answer may be rough but is reasonable.

Are All Estimates Good Ones?

After discussing the key characteristics of computational estimation, Jane started giving her children multiplication problems of two double-digit numbers for them to estimate. Among the first batch of problems was 54 × 32, and her children produced a whole gamut of different estimates, from 80, 150, to the ones we discussed in the previous section such as 1500, 1600, and 1800, and all the way to 15,000. Jane then said, "Since estimation isn't like calculating an exact answer, there may be many different answers. You all did a wonderful job in estimating this problem. Let's move on to the next."

It's true that there can be many different answers for estimating an arithmetic problem. However, not all of them are reasonable. Suppose you had a meal in a restaurant and decided to leave a tip of about 15%. After you were presented with the bill of $38.92, you quickly estimated that your tip should be around $6.00. Compared to the corresponding exact answer of $5.84, this was a close estimate. But if you came up with an estimate of $11.00 (about 88% more than what you intended), you probably would laugh at yourself for doing some lousy math. On the other hand, if you underestimated by about the same percentage and left a meager tip of $0.70, your waitress would probably feel unhappy. Either way, an estimate will stop being useful when it's off by quite a bit. Generally, a 40% cutoff line is considered a lenient criterion.[1] That is, if the exact answer of a problem is 100, a lenient criterion is to allow any estimates between 60 and 140 to be considered reasonable.

By this criterion, reasonable estimates for 54 × 32 are the ones between 1037 (40% below the exact answer of 1728) and 2419 (40% above). Those outside this range should be considered unreasonable, such as 80, 150, and 15,000, as they do not provide a useful frame of reference for solving a real-world problem such as tipping.

By failing to differentiate between reasonable estimates and unreasonable ones, Jane left her children the impression that they didn't need to strive to make their estimate reasonable as long as they came up with an estimate. In teaching this topic, a constructive way is to let your children know that not all estimates are good ones. At the beginning stage, you may make your criterion even more lenient than 40%—let's say 50%. After you get all answers, calculate the lower and upper limits for reasonable estimates and use these limits to see whose estimates are within the reasonable range. Gradually, you can raise the bar a little. If you want to emphasize the closeness of an estimate, you may adopt a more stringent criterion such as 30%. In doing such exercises, you may even select one or two children who produce the closest estimates as winners for each round.

The underlying idea is that, to be useful, estimates have to be reasonable, that is, not too far away from their corresponding exact answers.

How Practical Is an Estimate If It Takes 4 Minutes?

It was the second day of practice on estimating 2-digit multiplication problems, and Jane gave this direction to her fifth-grade children: "Here's a problem on the smartboard. You have four minutes to come up with an estimate. Then we'll share the results."

Four minutes is an awfully long time for fifth-grade children to produce an estimate for a 2-digit multiplication problem. In the previous section, it was mentioned that estimates should be reasonable in order to be useful. Here's an additional essential feature for estimates: They have to be produced in a relatively quick manner. Let's see why there should be a speediness factor involved in producing an estimate.

To address this issue, a question that should be answered first is: "What are estimates used for?"

Estimation is a useful tool both in and outside of the school setting. In doing school work, students may often use it to check if an answer obtained through exact calculation is reasonable, as a safeguard against careless errors. Even if calculators are used, sometimes a keystroke may not be pressed hard enough, or a series of operations may be executed in a different way than expected. If the answer obtained through exact calculation is very different from such an estimate, it's a good indication that some error may have been made and more careful calculations may be necessary.

Outside school, estimation is often called for in place of exact calculation because the latter in many situations is unnecessary. An example of this is estimating the amount of a tip in a restaurant, in which case a rough amount is usually sufficient.

Neither use of estimation is practical if it takes longer than exact calculation. Imagine that you are taking a formal timed test such as SAT, where you have only a limited time for each section. If it takes you 1 minute to manually calculate a problem, you probably wouldn't spend 2 minutes estimating the same problem in order to determine if you have made any possible careless errors. Likewise, for a real-world situation such as tipping in a restaurant, half a minute is usually sufficient to calculate the exact tip amount with paper and pencil. It is unimaginable that you would spend 4 minutes coming up with an estimate.

It's clear that in addition to the reasonableness criterion, there should be another criterion to judge the usefulness of an estimate: the speediness factor. Generally, an estimate should not take longer than the corresponding exact calculation. Thus, a formal definition of computational estimation, when all these factors are taken into consideration, can be given as: Computational estimation is the process of arriving at a rough but reasonable answer to an arithmetic problem in a relatively quick manner without resorting to any external calculating devices such as paper and pencil. In short, this definition stresses three main features of computational estimation: reasonable, quick, and obtained mentally.

A rule of thumb is that estimation shouldn't take longer than calculating the exact answer to the same problem. Most children need much less time than 4 minutes to precisely calculate a 2-digit by 2-digit, or 3-digit by 2-digit multiplication problem using paper and pencil. Therefore, Jane was giving her children too much time for estimating such a problem. Some children might use this time to mentally calculate an exact answer, as many elementary school children have a strong tendency to apply exact-answer oriented procedures in attempting an estimate. Limiting the time allowed may help force them out of this tendency.

Be Extremely Careful When Rounding 1-Digit Numbers

In teaching how to estimate a product, Jane gave her children this general rule: First round both factors to the nearest multiple of a power of 10, and then find the product of the rounded numbers. For practicing purposes, she gave the multiples of the few most common powers of 10 a number may be rounded to, as listed in the following Math in Action box.

 Math in Action: Multiples of the Few Most Common Powers of 10

- 10: 10, 20, 30, 40 . . . 90;
- 100: 100, 200, 300, 400 . . . 900;
- 1000: 1000, 2000, 3000, 4000 . . . 9000.

As an example, Jane said, 78 may be rounded to 80, 214 may be rounded to 200, and 6751 may be rounded to 7000, and so on.

Jane then handed out a worksheet and led her children in estimating the multiplication problems listed on it. The first problem was 351 × 6. By following her rule, her children came up with 351 × 6 ≈ 400 × 10 = 4000. Jane used a calculator and found the exact answer to this problem was 2106. Her intuition told her that an estimate of 4000 was just too high, but she couldn't figure out where the problem was.

We have previously talked about a criterion of 40% already being lenient, and an estimate of 4000 for 351 × 6 is about 90% off. Such an estimate is hardly of any use. Here let's develop a formula for exploring the effect of rounding on the size of the final product. For a multiplication problem, we may use error of rounding to refer to the ratio of the difference between the rounded and original factors with regard to the original factor. This error can be expressed as:

$$error\ of\ rounding = \frac{rounded\ number - original\ number}{original\ number} \times 100\%$$

where a positive result indicates that the number has been rounded up whereas a negative result indicates that the number has been rounded down.

For example, when 76 is rounded to 80, the error of rounding is $\frac{80-76}{76} \times 100\% = 5.3\%$. In other words, compared with the original number 76, the rounded number has been increased by about 5.3%. Similarly, rounding 214 to 200 yields an error of −6.5%.

When a 2- or 3-digit number is rounded to its nearest tens or hundreds, the error of rounding is usually low, as the previous examples show. However, when a 1-digit number is rounded, the error of rounding can be large due to the small size in the denominator in the formula. For example, although the difference between 80 and 76 is 4, and that between 10 and 6 is also 4, rounding 76 to 80 results in an error of a small 5.3% whereas the error in rounding 6 to 10 is as high as 66.7%.

As a general rule, be aware of size of rounding errors and try to keep them small. For this reason, be extremely careful when you round 1-digit numbers because that can potentially result in very large errors. This, of course, doesn't mean that you may not round 1-digit numbers at all. As an example, in estimating 8 × 674, you may round 8 up to 10 but round 674 down to 600 to compensate for the increase in rounding up 8 and still arrive at a reasonable estimate (8 × 674 = 5392, and the result of using 10 × 600 = 6000 is an overestimate of 11.3%).

There Is Often More Than One Way to Round a Number

In teaching how to estimate whole-number multiplication problems, Jane laid out the basic procedure that her children needed to follow: Round the two factors and then multiply the rounded factors. Then she gave them this rule for rounding 2- or 3-digit numbers: "When the ones digit is 4 or smaller, round this digit down to 0. If it's 5 or greater, round this digit up, that is, change it into 0 and increase the tens digit by 1. For example, 74 should be rounded down to 70, and 76 should be rounded up to 80."

This rule is fine for rounding for its own sake. Nevertheless, Jane was teaching her children how to estimate, and rounding as a part of the estimation process shouldn't be a separate procedure, but rather, should be executed in conjunction with consideration of the whole problem at hand. To use an example, in estimating 76 × 32, it makes good sense to round the two factors to 80 and 30, respectively, and obtain an estimate of 2400. This estimate, compared with the corresponding exact answer, 2432, is off by only 1.3%.

Now suppose 76 is used in a different problem, 76 × 128. By the procedure Jane told her children, an estimate could be obtained through 80 × 130 = 10400. However, both factors in the given problem are about the same distance from 100, one above and the other below. Rounding both factors to this common number may produce a faster result: 100 × 100 = 10000.

Not only would you obtain the second estimate faster, it was also a better estimate (76 × 128 = 9728). Let's use a formula to measure the error of estimation following the formula for error of rounding developed in the previous section (in fact, we used this formula indirectly but didn't elaborate on it when we were discussing the tipping problem). Basically, the error of estimation is the ratio of the difference between an estimate and the exact answer to the exact answer, expressed in percent. Informally, this is simply how much, and in what direction, an estimate deviates from the exact answer. This error can be expressed in the formula:

$$error\ of\ estimation = \frac{estimate - exact\ answer}{exact\ answer} \times 100\%$$

where a positive sign indicates an overestimate, and a negative sign an underestimate. Using this formula, we can obtain the first estimate's error to the problem 76 × 128 as $\frac{10400 - 9728}{9728} \times 100\% = 6.9\%$. Substituting 10000 for 10400 in the same formula will produce a smaller error of estimation: 2.8%.

To sum up, rounding as a part of the estimation process should be handled in conjunction with the whole problem instead of by itself. Otherwise it would give children the impression that there is only one way to round a number. How a number is rounded to solve an estimation problem may be impacted by several factors, and children need to take into consideration the specific features of the estimation problem at hand. After all, an estimate should be close to the exact answer enough to be useful and it should be solved in a relatively quick manner.

Note

1 I discussed this cutoff criterion in these articles: Liu, F. (2009). Computational estimation strategies on whole-number multiplication by third- and fifth-grade Chinese students. *School Science and Mathematics, 109*, 325–337; Liu, F. (2013). Are exact calculation and computational estimation categorically different? *Applied Cognitive Psychology, 27*, 672–682.

17

Odds and Ends

On different occasions, Jane uses some mathematical terms or formulations not quite the way they are meant to be used. A term describing a mathematical concept usually has specific denotations and may not be easily exchangeable with another term. Each of the following sections discusses such a case as indicated by its subtitle. The problematic words or phrases are underlined, with a corresponding formulation or words to use suggested, presented in italics. The last paragraph in each section gives an explanation why the original formulation or words are problematic and why they should be replaced with the suggested formulation.

Circumference

"The formula for finding the circumference of a circle is: $\underline{c = d\pi}$."
Formulation or words to use: $c = \pi d$.

Explanation: Letters, such as x, y, and z in English, are often used to represent any one of a set of numbers known as *variables*. As the term indicates, the quantity assumed by a variable may change from situation to situation (*variable* comes from *vary*, meaning "change"). A letter may also be used to represent a value that remains unchanged. Such a value is called a constant. π is such a constant. By mathematical convention, when a variable and a constant appear in the same term of a mathematical expression or formula, the constant is written first, followed by the variable, such as πd. If a numeral is also used, then it appears before either one, such as $2\pi r$. Again, this is only a matter of convention.

Clock Hands

> "Look at my clock here. The <u>red hand</u> is the hour hand. The <u>blue hand</u> is the minute hand."
> Formulation or words to use: *shorter hand*; *longer hand*

Explanation: The color used on an analog clock has nothing to do with distinguishing between the hour hand and minute hand. It's the length of the hands that does. While one manufacturer may make the hour hand red and minute hand blue, another manufacturer may very well make the two hands in opposite colors. Children conditioned to tell the two hands apart by color will have to relearn the true mechanism of distinguishing the two clock hands by their lengths. If you have a choice, choose model clocks having hands of the same color. That way children will be forced to look for what's intrinsic in what makes an hour hand an hour hand and what makes a minutes hand a minute hand.

Commas

> "Your answer for this problem is 6300. But there's something wrong here. You must write a comma for <u>every group of three digits</u>."
> Formulation or words to use: "Use a comma for every group of three digits for *numbers 10,000 or higher*."

Explanation: Commas aren't part of a number. They're used simply for easier recognition. When faced with a number of more than several digits written one after another without any commas, such as 1000000 or 12345678, people literally would have to count how many 0s or how many digits there are in it. In contrast, if commas are used, as in 1,000,000 or 12,345,678, readers can perceive its constituent digits at a glance without having to count. However, because they aren't an integral part of a number, commas don't have to be used if the perception of the number is easy. For example, many math textbooks and academic journals don't use commas for numbers composed of four digits, as in 6300. Commas do get used in numbers of more digits, but even here there're variations. Some journals use a narrow space, to the same effect, as in 63 000 000. The key point here is, if numbers with quite a few digits don't get used very frequently in children's school work, the use of commas doesn't have to be stressed or even required.

Diameter

"The diameter of a circle is <u>two radii</u> put together."
Formulation or words to use: The diameter is a *chord that passes through the center*.

Explanation: Although the diameter is indeed twice as long as the radius of a circle, defining it as two radii put together may lead to mistaking the two line segments as shown in Figure 17.1(a) for the diameter of the circle. The definition of a diameter should start with a chord, which is a line segment that connects any two points on the circle. The definition of a diameter, then, should capture this key feature: It's a line segment straight across through the center of the circle, as shown in Figure 17.1(b).

Equation

"Let's look at this <u>equation</u> here: 0.8 + 0.375 = . Who can tell me how we should set it up in a vertical form?"
Formulation or words to use: *problem*.

Explanation: An equation is a statement of equality of expressions. In other words, an equation involves two expressions joined together by an equal sign (=) indicating a relationship of equality between them. $3x + 4 = 10$ is an

Figure 17.1 Two Radii Put Together (a) Don't Necessarily Make a Diameter (b)

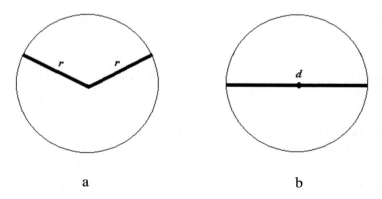

a   b

equation, and so is $4x^2 + 5x + 1 = 0$. For 0.8 + 0.35 = , there's only one expression on the left side of the equal sign, and there's no expression on the other side. Thus, it doesn't form an equality and it's not an equation. In such situations, we should simply say *problem* in place of *equation*.

Lines (1)

"A quadrilateral is a figure composed of four <u>lines</u>."
Formulation or words to use: *line segments.*

Explanation: In geometry, a line extends in both directions infinitely. Think of a number line. Any number, big or small, can be accommodated on it. In contrast, any one of the four sides of a quadrilateral doesn't extend beyond the vertices. Thus, it's only a portion of a line, delimited by two endpoints. Such a portion is called a *line segment.*

Lines (2)

"An angle is formed when two <u>lines</u> meet at a point."
Formulation or words to use: *rays.*

Explanation: A *ray* is part of a line that has one endpoint and extends in one direction infinitely. An *angle* is formed when two rays meet at their endpoints, and this common point is known as the *vertex*. In other words, neither side of the angle extends beyond the vertex, but it can extend in the other direction. An angle may also be formed by two line segments.

More Than

"Every place in a number is 10 <u>more than</u> the next place to its right."
Formulation or words to use: *times.*

Explanation: In the Hindu-Arabic numeration system, each place of a number has a specific value. These values are, from right to left, 1, 10, 100, 1000, and so on, with each one 10 *times* the previous one. For example, if we put a 7 in the hundreds place to make 700, it is 10 times the number formed by putting the same 7 in the tens place (70). The relationship of the two numbers joined by *times* is exactly what it is: multiplication ($700 = 10 \times 70$). In contrast, "more than" usually indicates an addition/subtraction relationship, as in "10 is 9 more than 1" ($10 = 9 + 1$; $10 - 1 = 9$).

Number

"Which <u>number</u> in 358 is in the tens place?"
"In 2719, which <u>number</u> is the largest? Which <u>number</u> is the smallest?"
"123, 213, and 321 all have the same <u>numbers</u>."
Formulation or words to use: *digit*.

Explanation: The Hindu-Arabic numeration system employs 10 symbols, namely, 1, 2, 3, 4, 5, 6, 7, 8, 9, and 0, to form numbers. For example, 358 is one *number*, which is composed of three *digits*: 3, 5, and 8. Similarly, 2719 is one *number*, and it is composed of four *digits*: 2, 7, 1, and 9. A number can be single-digit as well: Any one of the 10 digits can stand alone as a number.

Object

"Area is how much space a two-dimensional <u>object</u> has."
Formulation or words to use: *shape* or *figure*.

Explanation: All objects are three-dimensional. Area is two-dimensional, and that is probably what prompts Jane to say a "two-dimensional object." In defining area, resort to words that in themselves denote "two-dimensional," such as *shape* and *figure* suggest.

Percent

"A fraction can be changed into a percent by using this formula:

$$\frac{numerator}{denominator} = \frac{percent}{100} \text{."}$$

Formulation or words to use: $\dfrac{numerator}{denominator} = \dfrac{x}{100}$.

Explanation: A percent already has "over 100" in it, and it is incorrect to present a formula containing another "over 100." What appears in the position of "percent" in Jane's formula should actually be a variable representing only the numerator of the percent. If we want to change $\dfrac{3}{5}$ into a percent, for example, we can start by asking: "3/5 is what number over 100?", and this can be set up in an equation: $\dfrac{3}{5} = \dfrac{x}{100}$. Solving for x, we have:

$$5x = 3\,(100)$$
$$x = 60$$

Putting 60 in the position of x of the original equation, we have: $\dfrac{3}{5} = \dfrac{60}{100}$. As mentioned earlier in this book, a percent is no different from a fraction, and $\dfrac{60}{100}$ is virtually the answer we want to find. From this fraction, we just need to take a small step to transform it into the "percent" form, the one with a percentage sign: 60%.

Sphere

"The formula for the area of <u>spheres</u> is πr^2."
Formulation or words to use: *circles*.

Explanation: Figures or shapes drawn on a flat surface (plane) are often called 2-D geometric shapes. Geometric shapes that take up physical space (like objects) are referred to as 3-D geometric shapes or solids. A circle, like the image of the top of a round dining table, is a 2-D shape. The formula for calculating its area is πr^2. A sphere, like a basketball, is three-dimensional. 3-D shapes such as a rectangular prism may be composed of a number of faces and each face has its own area, and the term "surface area" is often used to refer to the sum of the areas of all its faces. The formula for calculating the surface area of a sphere is different from that for calculating the area of a circle.

Times

"More digits in a decimal don't necessarily mean a larger number. For example, 0.214 is smaller than 0.8. In fact, 0.213 is about four <u>times smaller than</u> 0.8."
Formulation or words to use: (*one fourth*) *of*

Explanation: *Times* means "multiplied by" and is readily translatable into a mathematical expression, as "3 times 4 is 12" is translatable into "$3 \times 4 = 12$." When we compare two numbers where one is several times the other, we can say similar things such as "18 is three times larger than 6," which can be translated into $18 = 3 \times 6$. However, "smaller than" cannot be used in the same way. Let's suppose what Jane said was (to make it easier to explain) "2 is four times smaller than 8." If we want to write this statement into a mathematical expression, we would have: $2 = 4 \times 8$, which we know is not correct. To fit into the equation $2 = \_\_ \times 8$, only one fourth (1/4) will work. So the correct way of saying what was intended is "0.213 is about one fourth of 0.8."

Units for Area and Volume

"When you calculate the area of a geometric figure, remember the unit of measure has an exponent 2. For example, a rectangle of 3 centimeters long and 5 centimeters wide has an area of 15 centimeters *squared*."
Formulation or words to use: <u>square</u> (centimeters).

Explanation: Although the exponent 2 in algebra is often read as "squared" (used as a verb), as $a^2 + b^2 = c^2$ is often read as "a squared plus b squared equals c squared," a unit of measure with the exponent 2 indicating area is a little different. By convention, it's read as "square" preceding the base measure. For example, the area of the aforementioned rectangle has an area of 15 *square* centimeters. Here *square* is used as an adjective. Similarly, there's an adjective for units of volume. A rectangular prism with dimensions of 2 cm, 4 cm, and 5 cm has a volume of 40 *cubic* centimeters (2 cm × 4 cm × 5 cm = 40 cm³). Usually it's not read as "40 centimeters cubed."

Appendix

Suggestions for Using *Common Mistakes in Teaching Elementary Math* with Study Groups

While readers may find this book a perfect resource guide and use it individually as they progress through the school year, it may serve as a book for study groups equally well. If you are a principal or instructional coach acting as facilitator of such a group consisting of teachers in your building, you may find the following steps easy to implement and yet highly effective. Such study sessions will have a direct, positive impact on your faculty's daily teaching of some fundamental math content, which, in turn, will lead to better student performance.

Because all sections in this book are structurally similar—namely, each section begins with Jane saying something problematic, followed by analysis of what she said and then advice on how to avoid making this mistake—a group study session may be conducted by following these steps:

1. Decide on a topic discussed in the book that fits the grade level of and is of particular interest to your group members as a whole.
2. Show on a smartboard Jane's way of presenting that specific topic. Ask if any of your group members teach the same way as Jane does and, if so, why it is problematic to teach that way.
3. Set aside about 20 or 30 minutes for reading the analysis part of the selected section.
4. Start a roundtable discussion on the ill effects of presenting the content in Jane's way. Have your group members reflect on how to avoid making such mistakes in their own teaching.
5. Resume reading, this time the advice part of the selected section. Ask your group members if they have come up with, while reflecting, the same strategy as suggested in the book or share their strategies if they have come up with different ones.

You may want to ask your group members to not read the selected section ahead of time. A discussion with varied opinions on whether Jane's way of teaching is problematic and why or why not it is so can be lively and thus its effect will be maximal. Such a desired effect may not be as easy to achieve when all members already have consensus on the issue being discussed.

Here are two examples.

Example 1

The following paragraph is from the beginning of "Don't Ever Say 'Subtract the Smaller Number from the Larger One'" in Chapter 4 (p. 27):

> This is what Jane did in her classroom one day. She presented a 1-digit subtraction problem, 9 − 4, to her children and said, "Let's solve this problem. Now subtract the smaller number from the larger number. Tell me your answer."

Project the paragraph quoted on a smartboard. Lead the group discussion by asking these questions:

1. Is there anything problematic with what Jane said? Why or why not?
2. (If different opinions on this question have been voiced) Can you convince those holding the opposite idea from yours of why you think it's (or not) problematic to say that?
3. Can you say something similar in division, as "For 12 ÷ 6, divide the larger number by the smaller number"?

After some discussion on these questions, possibly with different opinions expressed, devote about 30 minutes to reading the analysis part of the chosen section (pp. 27–28).

Before assigning the last part of the advice section, you may also want to conduct some discussion first. Pose such questions as:

◆ Now that we know what Jane said is problematic, can you suggest a proper way of explaining how to solve this problem?
◆ How can you avoid this way of teaching in the future?

Example 2

The following problem is from the beginning of "Aunt Sally Is Evil—The Order of Operations" in Chapter 7 (p. 54):

7 − 2 + 3 = ?

Here's a suggested sequence of steps for conducting the group study on this topic:

1. Pass a pencil and a small piece of paper to each group member.
2. Project the example problem (7 − 2 + 3 = ?) on the smartboard and ask your group members to solve it without using a calculator, searching on the Internet, or consulting with each other. Ask them to write the answer on the paper just distributed. Half a minute is sufficient.
3. Collect all the pieces of paper. If there are six, seven, or more members in your study group, it is likely that while most members will arrive at the correct answer, a few may get it wrong.
4. Ask those who got the wrong answer to justify what they got, and this will invariably lead to the mention of "PEMDAS" or "Please Excuse My Dear Aunt Sally."
5. Start book reading. Devote about 30 minutes to reading, individually, the analysis part of this section (pp. 54–56, from "But the right answer is not 2" till "you got the picture").
6. As added proof, project the screen of a calculator showing the execution of 7 − 2 + 3 =. Most calculators designed for students, such as TI-15 or higher models, are good to use, but avoid using any primitive-type ones, usually the size of a sticky note or even smaller (such calculators may execute operations in a from-left-to-right manner because they do not have sufficient memory).
7. Ask if the mnemonic "PEMDAS" is the primary reason for arriving at the wrong answer for 7 − 2 + 3 =.
8. Go back to the reading of the book, this time focusing on the last section, on how to avoid making this mistake (p. 56).
9. Suggest these topics for discussion:
   - Why did "PEMDAS" lead some people to the wrong answer?
   - What effect does "PEMDAS" have on children if they are told this is the order of operations?
   - What's the key difference between "PEMDAS" and the actual rules concerning the order of operations, presented on page 56?

–   Can you solve the problems presented in the Math in Action boxes on pages 56–57 using these rules?

   –   What lessons can you draw with regard to creating your own mnemonics on some mathematical rules?

All the other sections in this book can be handled in a similar manner. The idea is, discourage your group members from reading the selected section ahead of time such that the discussion will be more effective than when there is consensus. For a few sections, though, a little preparation on topics for discussion other than what's suggested in this appendix may be necessary.